HARD PRESS
NET

ISBN: 9781313140836

Published by:
HardPress Publishing
8345 NW 66TH ST #2561
MIAMI FL 33166-2626

Email: info@hardpress.net
Web: http://www.hardpress.net

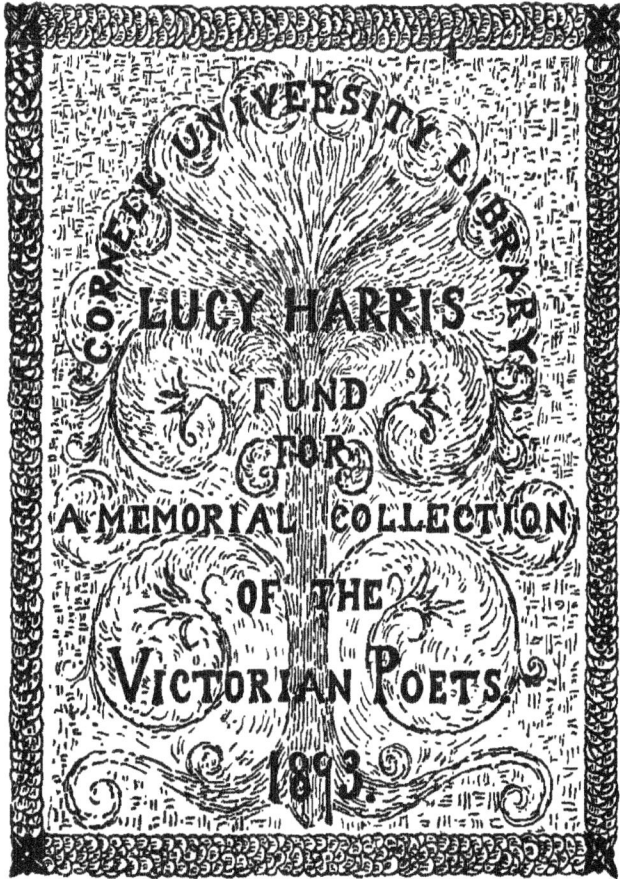

EROS AND PSYCHE.

EROS & PSYCHE

A POEM IN TWELVE MEASURES

BY

ROBERT BRIDGES

THE STORY DONE IN-
TO ENGLISH FROM THE
LATIN OF APULEIUS

Esce di mano a Lui che la vagheggia
Prima che sia, a guisa di fanciulla
Che piangendo e ridendo pargoleggia,
L'anima semplicetta che sa nulla,
Salvo che, mossa da lieto Fattore,
Volentier torna a ciò che la trastulla.

LONDON: GEORGE BELL AND SONS
1885

A76:763

CHISWICK PRESS:—C. WHITTINGHAM AND CO., TOOKS COURT, CHANCERY LANE.

MEASURE I.

1.

IN midmost length of hundred-citied
　　　Crete,
　　The land that cradled Zeus, of old renown;
Where first Demeter nurseried her wheat,
And Minos fashioned Law, ere he went down
To judge the shrinking hordes of Hell's domain;
There dwelt a King on the Omphalian plain
Eastward of Ida, in a little town.

2.

Three daughters had this King, of whom my tale
Time hath preserved, that loveth to despise
The wealth which men misdeem of much avail,
Their glories for themselves that they devise;
For clerkly is he, old hard-featured Time,
And poets' fabled song, and lovers' rhyme
He storeth on his shelves to please his eyes.

B

3.

These three princeſses all were fairest fair ;
And of the elder twain 'tis truth to say
That if they stood not quite above compare,
Yet in their prime they bore the palm away,
Outwards of lovelineſs ; but Nature's mood,
Gracious to make, had grudgingly endued
And marred by gifting ill the beauteous clay.

. .

4.

And being in honour they were well content
To feed on lovers' looks and courtly smiles,
To hang their necks with jewelled ornament,
And gold, that vanity in vain beguiles,
And live in gaze, and take their praise for due,
To be the peerleſs fairest then to view
Within the shores of Greece and all her isles.

5.

But of that youngest one, the third princeſs,
There is no likeneſs ; since she was as far
Removed from beauty as is uglineſs,

Though on the side where heavenly wonders are,
Ideals out of being and above,
Which music worships,. but if love should love,
'Tis, as the poet saith, to love a star.

6.

Her vision rather drave from pafsion's heart
What earthly soil it had afore pofsefsed ;
Since to man's purer unsubstantial part
The brightnefs of her presence was addrefsed :
And such as scoffed at God, when once they saw
Her heavenly glance were shamed and stood in awe,
And turned to things unseen and praised the Best.

7.

And so before her, wheresoe'er she went,
Stilling the crowd a sacred whisper ran ;
And voices hushed, heads bowed, and knees were bent
And hands upraised ; and thence this tale began,
That Love's own mother had come down on earth
Sweet Cytherea, or a wondrous birth
Had given an equal Goddefs unto man.

8.

Then Aphrodite's statue in its place
Stood clear of worshippers; if Cretans prayed
For beauty or for children, love or grace,
Their vows and prayers were offered to the maid;
Unto the maid their hymns of praise were sung,
Their victims bled for her, for her were hung
Their garlands, heaped their gifts, and none forbade.

9.

And thence opinion spread beyond the shores,
From isle to isle the wonder flew, it came
Acrofs the Ægæan on a thousand oars,
And furthest lands echoed the virgin's fame;
Until throughout all Greece the foamborn queen
Was scarce adored, or paid with rites so mean
As rather served the more to seal her shame.

10.

No longer to high Paphos now 'twas sailed;
The fragrant altar by the Graces served
Was nigh of men forsaken; pilgrims failed

The rocky island to her name reserved,
Proud Ephyra, and Meropis renowned;
'Twas all for Crete her votaries were bound
To swell the allegiance from her rule that swerved.

11.

Which when in heaven great Aphrodite saw,
Who is the breather of the year's bright morn,
Fount of desire and beauty without flaw,
And doth the life that she creates adorn;
Seeing that without her generative might
Nothing can spring upon the shores of light,
Nor aught that tastes of joy or love be born;

12.

She, when she saw the insult, did not hide
Her anger, but impatient in her rage
Pondered what punishment might best o'erride
The mimic minion of her heritage.
For still her beauty, though 'twas known the first
Of beauty was with jealousy accurst;
And well she loved revenge, and thus gan chide.

13.

" Not long, I wot, shall that poor girl of Crete
God it in my despite : I soon will bring
Such mischief on the sickly counterfeit
As quite shall cure her tribe of worshipping ;
For I will smite her in the way which most
Shall cast to shameful scorn her beauty's boast
And leave her long alive to feel the sting."

14.

With that she calls to her her comely boy,
The limber scion of the God of War,
The fruit adulterous, which for man's annoy
To that fierce partner Cytherea bore,
Eros, the ever young, who only grew
In mischief, and was Cupid named anew
In westering aftertime of poets' lore.

15.

What the first dawn of manhood is, the time
Of flush and juice, the bursting-ripe content
Of full growth lusty on the goal of prime,

That onward ecstasy the gods forwent ;
Such Eros seemed in years, and is portrayed,
Trifler for lack of sorrow, joy delayed
Upon the brink of spending, never spent.

16.

His skin is brilliant with the ichorous flood
That swiftly to his veins leaps from his heart,
Hotter than fire and redder far than blood ;
From out his eyes small flames in flashes dart.
His head is thick with curls of golden hair ;
His tongue as honey, and his face most fair,
But wantonneſs betrays in every part.

17.

He goeth naked, but with sprightly wings
Red iridescent are his shoulders fledged.
His weapons are a bow he deftly strings,
And little arrows barbed and keenly edged ;
And these he shooteth true ; but else the youth
For all his seeming recketh nought of truth,
And most deceives where most he standeth pledged

He 'tis that makes of love a bitter strife,
Using the eager joys of men's desire
For baits and lures, until their silly life
Consumed away, of folly they expire.
For all he promiseth is aye denied ;
Nor truest tears have ever satisfied
The cruel boy, nor quenched his kindled fire.

19.

'Tis he who frights kind sleep from lovers' eyes,
And prints the early wrinkles on their brows ;
And in their hearts unnumbered jealousies,
And all contrary pafsions will arouse.
And night and day, unseen in every town
From house to house he flitteth up and down,
And turns to sport the seal of wifely vows.

20.

Him then she called, and gravely kifsing told
The strange dishonour to her godhead done ;
And how, if he from that in heaven would hold,

On earth he must maintain it as her son :
The rather that his weapons were most fit,
As was his skill most rare to champion it ;
And flattering thus his ready zeal she won.

21.

Whereon she quickly led him down on earth,
And showed him Psyche, thus the maid was named ;
Whom when she showed, but could not hide her worth,
She grew with anger tenfold more enflamed.
"But if" she cried "thou smite her as I bid,
Our glory soon shall of this stain be rid,
And she and all her likes for ever shamed.

22.

"Make her to love the loathliest, basest wretch,
Deformed in body, and of moonstruck mind,
A hideous brute and vicious, born to fetch
Anger from dogs and cursing from the blind.
And let her pafsion for the monster be
As shamelefs and detestable as he
Is most extreme and vile of humankind."

23.

Which said, when he agreed, she spake no more,
But left him to his task, and took her way
Beside the ripples of the shell-strewn shore,
The southward stretching margin of a bay,
Whose sandy curves she pafsed, and taking stand
Upon its taper horn of furthest land,
Looked left and right to rise and set of day.

24.

Fair was the sight ; for now though full an hour
The sun had sunk she saw a wondrous light
In shifting colour to the zenith tower,
And grow more gorgeous ever and more bright.
Bathed in the warm and comfortable glow,
The fair delighted queen forgot her woe,
And watched the unwonted pageant of the night.

25.

Broad and low down, where last the sun had been,
A wealth of orange gold was thickly shed,
And touching that a curtain pale of green,

Like apples are before their rinds grow red :
Then to the height the variable hue
Of rose and pink and crimson freaked with blue,
And olive-bordered clouds o'er lilac led.

26.

High in the opposèd west the wondering moon
All silvery green in flying green was fleeced ;
And round the blazing South the splendour soon
Caught all the heaven, and ran to North and East ;
And Aphrodite knew this thing was wrought
By great Poseidon, and she took the thought
She would go see with whom he kept his feast.

27.

Swift to her wish came swimming on the waves
His lovely ocean nymphs, her guides to be,
The Nereids all, who live among the caves
And valleys of the deep, Cymodocè,
Agavè, blue-eyed Hallia and Nesæa
Speio, and Thoë, Glaucè and Actæa,
Iaira, Melitè and Amphinomè,

28.

Apseudès and Nemertès, Callianafsa,
Cymothoë, Thaleia, Limnorrhæa,
Clymenè, Ianeira and Ianafsa,
Doris and Panopè and Galatæa,
Dynamenè, Dexamenè and Maira,
Ferusa, Doto, Proto, Callianeira,
Amphithoë, Oreithuia and Amathæa.

29.

And after them sad Melicertes drave
His chariot, that with swift unfellied wheel,
By his two dolphins drawn along the wave,
Flew as they plunged, yet did not dip nor reel,
But like a plough that sheers the heavy land
Stood on the flood, and back on either hand
O'erturned the briny furrow with its keel.

30.

Behind came Tritons, that their conches blew,
Greenbearded, tailed like fish, all sleek and stark ;
And hippocampi tamed, a bristly crew,

The browzers of old Proteus' weedy park ;
And certain Tritons brought a shell for boat,
And setting void its hollow fan afloat,
Pushed it to shore and bade the queen embark :

31.

And then the goddefs stepped upon the shell
Which took her weight; and others drew a train
Of soft silk over her, which soon gan swell
In sails, at breath of flying zephyrs twain ;
And all her way with foam in laughter strewn,
With stir of music and of conches blown,
Was Aphrodite launched upon the main.

MEASURE II.

1.

BUT in the house of Psyche there was woe,
    Such as displeasure of the Gods will
       bring,
When they spy cause for jealousy, although
Man's foolish heart be witlefs of the thing.
For Psyche's cheer fell, swifter than decline
Of lovelorn maids, when out of cure they pine;
And melancholy fastened on the King.

2.

Already in good time her sisters both,
Whose honest charms were never framed as hers,
Had unto royal lovers plighted troth,

The noblest of a crowd of courtiers;
But she, the more that she was praised above
Them whom men loved, lacked yet the more their love,
And gained but number to her worshippers.

3.

To see her sisters' joy had been her lot,
And now that they were gone her heart would brood
Upon the blifs her greater grace o'ershot,
Prisoned at home in peerlefs solitude.
Nay, if her beauty could have been the price
Of some plain peasant's love, such sacrifice
She not had shunned, nor scorned the boon so rude.

4.

" For what is beauty if it doth not fire
The loving answer of man's eager soul ?
Since 'tis the native food of fond desire,
Which doth for good our various world control,
And if it failed, life hath no other source,
No perpetuity, no stir, no force,
No bettering rivalry, nor aim, nor goal.

5.

" And though there yet be things, whose matchlefs
worth
And heavenly function writ above our sense,
Lie waste and disregarded on the earth
By reason of our grofs intelligence;
These things man calls not beauteous now, although
It live in nature's scheme that he should grow
In time to gather satisfaction thence.

6.

" But to be praised for beauty and denied
The meed of beauty, this was yet unknown :
Since men were men, the best have ever vied
To win the fairest women for their own ;
And though their coveting hath oft reversed
The hope of nature's dower, I yet am first
Whom beauty hath procured to live alone."

7.

Thus would she reason, to soft tears and sighs
Then falling, while she moaned her joylefs state ;
Whom when her sire, in such distracted guise

Saw, nor himself was inscient of fate,
Then of his sorrow he the Gods accused,
And sought if remedy might yet be used
To avert their anger or propitiate.

8.

For round his palace like ill-omened birds
He might see gathered soothsayers and seers,
Whose omens, auguries, and riddling words,
Reached in unwelcome whisper to his ears,
With portents happed, and prodigies that shewed
Strange fates, and aye some heaven-sent ill to bode
Unto his house ; whereat grew fixed his fears.

9.

So forth himself he set, and journeying went
To great Apollo's shrine, the Pythian ;
Where when the god he questioned if 'twas meant
That Psyche should be wed, and to what man,
The tripod shook, and o'er the vaporous well
The chaunting Pythoneſs gave oracle,
And thus in measured verse the sentence ran :

c

10.

High on the topmost rocks with funeral feast
Convey and leave the maid nor look to find
A mortal husband, but a savage beast,
The viperous scourge of gods and humankind;
Who shames and vexes all, and as he flies
With sword and fire Zeus trembles in the skies,
And groans arise from souls to hell consigned.

11.

Which words at heart, in travel slow and sad
The King returned ; nor yet could understand
The bitter bidding he for answer had,
Nor yet make question of the plain command.
And all his mournful council day by day
Sat unresolved, fearing to disobey,
And still in fear to take the woe in hand.

12.

Some said that she to Talos was devote,
The metal giant, who with mile-long stride
Covered the isle, walking around by rote

Thrice every day at his appointed tide;
Who shepherded the sea-goats on the coast,
And as he pafsed caught up, and live would roast,
Prefsing them 'gainst his burning ribs and side :

13.

Whose head was made of fine gold beaten work,
Of silver pure his arms and gleaming chest,
Thence of green-bloomèd bronze far as the fork,
Of iron weather-rusted all the rest.
One single vein he had, which pafsing down
From head to foot was open in his crown,
And closèd by a nail ; such was this pest.

14.

But when no longer fate might be delayed,
And solemnly her sire began ordain
The pomp of death for bridal of the maid,
The torches, garlands and funereal wain,
With which must Psyche go by fate compelled
To meet that demon spouse, and she beheld
The fearful ceremony put in train,

15.

Then spake she to the King and said " O Sire,
Why wilt thou veil those venerable eyes
With piteous tears, which must of me require
More tears again than for myself arise?
Then, on the day my beauty first o'erstepped
Its mortal place it had been well to have wept;
But now the fault beyond our ruing lies.

16.

" That was my crime; the sentence is decreed,
And wherefore should we shrink from the award,
Or shun this bridegroom of immortal breed,
If none escape him with his fire and sword?
Rather, if I be willing, it may be
He will be generous; as 'tis sure that he
In being my only lover, is my lord.

17.

" As to be worshipped was my whole undoing,
So my submifsion must the forfeit pay:
And welcome were the morning of my wooing,

Tho' after it should dawn no other day.
Up to the mountains! for I heard the voice
Of my deliverance on the winds, *Rejoice,*
Rejoice, arise, my Psyche, and come away ! "

18.

With such distempered speech, which little cheered
Her mourning house, she went to choose with care
The raiment for her day of wedlock weird
Her body as for burial to prepare ;
Nor spared her sire in pious hope to make
The sacrifice, if yet for pity's sake
Or Zeus or Hera might attend his prayer.

19.

After whose marriage, as the perfect rite,
Were Cretans wedded : and from out the stream
Where Hera bathed—Tethrys or Theron hight—
Upon the evening of her fate supreme,
Thence fetched they water for the bride, and more
In funeral urns stood by her father's door,
Joining with nuptial rites the rites extreme.

20.

They set on high upon the bridal wain
Her bed for bier, and yet no corpse thereon ;
But like as when unto a warrior slain
And not brought home the ceremonies done
Are empty, for afar his body brave
Lies lost, deep buried by the wandering wave,
Or neath the foes his fury fell upon,

21

So was her hearse : and with it went afore,
Singing the solemn dirge that moves to tears,
The singers; and behind, clad as for war,
The nobles of the isle, princes and peers,
All neath their armour robed in linen white ;
And in their left were shields, and in their right
Torches they bore aloft instead of spears.

22.

With them the father, his grey head bent low,
Followed uncrowned, like one condemned to die,
That braves at heart his being's overthrow,

While slavishly his feet thereto comply,
And willing seem for only lack of will :
But life, with all he loved and loveth still,
Melts as a dream doth on an open eye.

23.

And next the virgin tribe in white forth sailed,
With flowery wreaths in hand ; and midst of those
Went Psyche, all in lily-whitenefs veiled,
With chaplet of the white Cydonian rose.
And last the common folk, a weeping crowd,
Far as the city gates with wailings loud
Followed, and filled the sad procefsion's close.

24.

Thus forth and up the mount they went, until
The funeral chariot must be left behind,
Since road was none for steepnefs of the hill ;
And slowly by the narrow path they wind :
All afternoon their white and scattered file
Toiled on distinct, ascending many a mile
Over the long brown slopes and crags unkind.

25.

But ere unto the snowy peak they came
Of that stormshapen pyramid so high,
'Twas evening, and with footsteps slow and lame
They gathered up their lagging company :
And then her sire, even as Apollo bade,
Set on the topmost rock the haplefs maid,
With trembling hands and melancholy cry.

26.

There left they her, turning with sad farewells
To haste their homeward course, as best they might :
But night was crowding up the barren fells,
And hid full soon their rocky path from sight ;
And each unto his stumbling foot to hold
His torch was fain, for o'er the moon was rolled
A mighty cloud from heaven, to blot her light.

27.

And through the darknefs for long while was seen
That armoured train with waving fires to thread
Downwards, by pafs, defile, and black ravine,

Each leading on the way that he was led.
Slowly they gained the plain, and one by one
Into the shadows of the woods were gone,
Or in the clinging mists were quenched and fled.

28.

But unto Psyche, pondering o'er her doom
In tearful silence on her stony chair,
A zephyr straying out of heaven's wide room
Rushed down, and gathering round her unaware
Seized her deep-bosomed vesture fast in hold
And, like a ship, when its white sails unfold,
Wafted her forth upon the tranquil air.

29.

Swiftly he sped her off, with swimming brain
And airy joy, along the mountain side,
Till, hid from earth by ridging summits twain,
They came upon a valley deep and wide:
Where the strong Zephyr with his burden sank,
And laid her down upon a grafsy bank,
Mong thyme and violets and daisies pied.

30.

And straight upon the touch of that sweet bed
Both woe and wonder melted fast away :
And sleep with gentle strefs her sense o'erspread,
Gathering as darknefs doth on drooping day.
And nestling to the ground, she slowly drew
Her wearied limbs together, and, ere she knew,
Wrapt in forgetfulnefs and slumber lay.

MEASURE III.

1.

AFTER long sleep when Psyche first
    awoke,
  A smile delayed the opening of her eyes,
Fed from the comfort of her spirit, that spoke
Delighted invitation to arise.
But soon the encompafsment of sights so strange
Rebuffed her mood, nor could she piece the change,
But lay awhile embarrafsed with surprise.

2.

Anon her quickening thought took up its task,
And all came back as it had happed o'ernight;
The sad procefsion of the wedding mask,
The melancholy toiling up the height,
The solitary rocks where she was left;
And thence in dark and airy waftage reft,
How on the flowers she had been disburdened light.

3.

Thereafter she would rise and see what place
That voyage had its haven in, and found
She stood upon a little hill, whose base
Shelved off into the valley all around ;
And all round that the steep cliffs rose away,
Save on one side where to the break of day
The widening dale withdrew in falling ground.

4.

There, out from over sea, and scarce so high
As she, the sun above his watery blaze
Upbroke the grey dome of the morning sky,
And struck the island with his level rays ;
Sifting his gold thro' lazy mists, that still
Climbed on the shadowy roots of every hill,
And in the tree-tops breathed their silvery haze.

5.

At hand on either side there was a wood ;
And on the upward lawn, that sloped between,
Not many paces back a temple stood,

By even steps ascending from the green ;
With shafts and pediments of marble made,
It filled the paſsage of the rising glade,
And there withstayed the sun in dazzling sheen.

6.

Too fair for human art, so Psyche thought,
It might the fancy of some god rejoice ;
Like to those halls which lame Hephæstos wrought,
Original, for each god to his choice,
In high Olympus ; where his matchleſs lyre
Apollo wakes, and the responsive choir
Of Muses sing alternate with sweet voice.

7.

Wondering she drew anigh, and in a while
Went up the steps as she would entrance win,
And faced her shadow 'neath the peristyle
Upon the golden gate, whose flanges twin—
As there she stood, irresolute at heart
To try—swung to her of themselves apart ;
Whereat she paſsed between and stood within.

8.

A foursquare court it was with marble floored,
Enclosed about with pillared porticoes,
That echoed in a somnolent accord
The music of a fountain, which arose
Sparkling in air, and splashing in its tank ;
Whose note of pleasure, as it swelled or sank,
Gave idle voice to silence and repose.

9.

Thro' doors beneath the further colonnade,
Panelled with pictured bronze and burnished gold,
The riches of the chambers were displayed :
And, standing in the court, she might behold
Cedar, and silk, and silver ; and that all
The pargeting of ceiling and of wall
Was frescoed o'er with figures manifold.

10.

Then making bold to go within, she heard
A gentle speech of welcome in her ear ;
And seeing none that could have spoken word,

She waited : when again *Lady, draw near ;*
Enter ! was cried ; and now more voices came
From all the air around calling her name,
And bidding her rejoice and have no fear.

11.

And one, if she would rest, would show her bed,
Made fresh for sleep with fragrant linen fine;
One, were she hungry, had a table spread
Like as the high gods have it when they dine :
Or, would she bathe, were those would heat the bath ;
The joyous cries contending in her path,
Psyche they said, *What wilt thou ? all is thine.*

12.

Then Psyche would have thanked their service true,
But that she feared her echoing words might scare
Those sightlefs tongues; and well by dream she knew
The voices of the mefsengers of prayer,
Which fly upon the gods' commandment, when
They answer the supreme desires of men,
Or for a while in pity hush their care.

13.

'Twas fancy's consummation, and because
She would do joy no curious despite,
She made not question how the wonder was;
Only concerned to take her full delight.
So to the bath, finding the best excuse
For eyelefs ministry in such a use,
She followed with the voice she heard invite.

14.

There being deliciously refreshed, from soil
Of earth made pure by water, fire, and air,
They clad her in soft robes of Asian toil,
Scented, that in her queenly wardrobe were;
And led her forth to dine, and all around
Sang as they served, the while the choral sound
Of strings unseen and reeds the burden bare.

15.

Pathetic strains and pafsionate they wove,
Urgent in ecstasies of heavenly sense;
Responsive rivalries, that, while they strove,

Combined in full harmonious suspense,
Entrancing wild desire, then fell at last
Lulled in soft closes, and with gay contrast
Launched forth their fresh unwearied excellence.

16.

Now Psyche, when her twofold feast was o'er,
Would feed her eye ; and choosing for her guide
A low-voiced singer, bade her come explore
The wondrous house ; until on every side
As surfeited with beauty, and seeing nought
But what was rich and fair beyond her thought,
And all her own, thus to the voice she cried :

17.

" Am I indeed a goddefs, or is this
But to be dead ; and through the gates of death
Pafsing unwittingly doth man not mifs
Body nor memory nor living breath ;
Nor by demerits of his deeds is cast,
But, paid with the desire he holdeth fast,
Is holp with all his heart imagineth ? "

D

18.

But her for all reply the wandering tongue
Called to the chamber where her bed was laid,
With broidered coverlets, and curtains hung :
And round the walls were everywhere displayed,
Between the gold pilasters laurel-crowned,
Each in its place, Love's victories renowned
Over the Gods, with wondrous art portrayed.

19.

Here Zeus, in likeneſs of a tawny bull,
Stooped on the Cretan shore his mighty knee,
While off his back Europa beautiful
Stepped pale against the blue Carpathian sea.
And here Apollo, as he caught amazed
Daphne, for lo ! her hands shot forth upraised
With leaves, her feet were rooted like a tree.

20.

Here Dionysos, springing from his car
At sight of Ariadne ; here upleapt
Adonis to the chase, breaking the bar

Of Aphrodite's arm for love who wept:
He spear in hand with leashèd dogs at strain;
A marvellous work.   But Psyche soon grown fain
Of rest, betook her to her bed and slept.

21.

Nor long had slept, when at a sudden stir
She woke; and one, that through the dark made way,
Was through the chamber door, and over her
The curtains rustled round her where she lay.
Then Psyche feared and trembled above need,
For 'twas her husband, by the fates decreed,
Who called her now by name, and kiſsed in play.

22.

His face and figure though she could not see,
She wished not then nor asked what night denied :
He was the lover she had lacked, and she,
Loving his loving, was his willing bride.
O'erjoyed she slept again ; but when anon
She woke at break of morning, he was gone ;
Only his empty place lay by her side.

23.

So all that day she spent in company
Of those soft voices ; and *Of right*, they said,
Art thou our Lady now. Be happily
Thy bridal morrow by thy servants sped.
But she but longed for night, again to taste
Her lover's lips ; and he in self-same haste
Came with the dark, and in the darkneſs fled.

24.

And thus the time went by ; for every night
He came, and though his name she never learned,
Nor was his image yielded to her sight
At morn or eve, she neither looked nor yearned
Beyond the joy she had : and custom brought
An ease to pleasure ; nor would Psyche's thought
Have ever to her earthly home returned,

25.

But that one night he said " Psyche, my soul,
Sad danger threatens us : thy sisters twain
Come to the mountain top, whence I thee stole,

And thou wilt hear their voices thence complain.
Answer them not: for know 'twill end our love
If they should hear or spy thee from above."
And Psyche said "Their cry shall be in vain."

26.

But being again alone, she thought 'twas hard
On her own blood; and blamed her joy as thief
Of theirs, her comfort which their comfort barred;
When she their care should be their care's relief.
All day she brooded on her father's woe,
And when at night her lover kifsed her, lo!
Her tender face was wet with tears of grief.

27.

Then questioned why she wept, she all confefsed;
And begged of him she might but once go nigh
To set her sire's and sisters' fears at rest.
Till he for pity could not but comply:
"Only if they should ask thee of thy love
Discover nothing to their ears above."
And Psyche said "In vain shall be their cry."

28.

And yet next day no sooner was alone,
Than she for lonelineſs her promise rued:
That having so much pleasure for her own,
'Twas all unshared and spent in solitude.
And when at night her love flew to his place,
More than afore she shamed his fond embrace,
And piteously with tears her plaint renewed.

29.

The more he now denied, the more she wept;
Nor would in anywise be comforted,
Unleſs her sisters, on the Zephyr swept,
Should in those halls be one day bathed and fed,
And see themselves the palace where she reigned.
And he by force of tears at last constrained,
Granted her wish unwillingly, and said:

30.

" Much to our peril hast thou won thy will;
Thy sisters' love, seeing thee honoured so,
Will sour to envy, and with jealous skill

Will pry to learn the thing thou must not know.
Answer not, nor enquire; for know that I
The day thou seest my face far hence shall fly,
And thou anew to bitterest fate must go."

31.

But Psyche said " Thy love is more than life,
Having thee thus leaves nothing to be won :
For should the noonday prove me to be wife
Even of the beauteous Eros, who is son
Of Cypris, I could never love thee more."
Whereat he fondly kifsed her o'er and o'er,
And peace was 'twixt them till the night was done.

MEASURE IV.

1.

AND truly need there was to that old King
For consolation : since the mournful day
Of Psyche's fate he took no comforting ;
But while for speedy death he still would pray
He hasted to his end ; his hair grew white,
His body withered, and with sorrow's blight
His sense decayed, and so he pined away.

2.

Which when his daughters learnt, they both were
Comfort and solace to their sire to lend.   [quick
But as not seldom they who nurse the sick

Will take the malady from them they tend,
So happed it now; for they who failed to cheer
Grew sad themselves, and in that palace drear
Confirmed the misery they came to mend.

3.

And them their sire then bade that place go seek
Where Psyche had been left, if they might find
What monster held her on the savage peak,
Or if she there had died of hunger pined;
And, by wild eagles stripped, her scattered bones
Might still be gathered from the barren stones,
Or if her fate had left no trace behind.

4.

So just upon this time her sisters both
Climbed on the cliff that hung o'er Psyche's vale;
And finding there no sign, to leave were loth
Ere well afsured she lurked not within hail.
So calling loud her name " Psyche ! " they cried,
" Psyche, O Psyche ! " and when none replied
They sank upon the rocks to weep and wail.

5.

But Psyche heard their voices where she sat,
And summoning the Zephyr bade him fleet
Those mourners down unto the grafsy plat
Midst of her garden, where she had her seat.
Then from the dizzy steep the wondering pair
Came swiftly sinking on his buoyant air,
And stood upon the terrace at her feet.

6.

Upsprang she then, and kifsed them and embraced,
And said " Lo, here am I, I whom ye mourn.
I am not dead, nor tortured, nor disgraced,
But blest above all days since I was born.
Here is my home.   Enter, that ye may see
How little cause has been to grieve for me,
And my desertion on the rocks forlorn."

7.

So entering by the golden gate, or e'er
The marvel of their hither flight had waned,
Fresh wonder took them now, for everywhere

Their eyes that lit on beauty were enchained;
And Psyche's airy service, as she bade,
Performed its magic office, and displayed
The riches of the palace where she reigned.

8.

And through the perfumed chambers they were led,
And bathed therein; and after, set to sup,
Were upon dreamlike delicacies fed,
And wine more precious than its golden cup.
Till seeing nothing lacked, and nought was theirs,
Their happinefs fell from them unawares,
And bitter envy in their hearts sprang up.

9.

And last, one said " Psyche, since not alone
Thou livest here in joy, as well we wot,
Who is the man who should these wonders own,
Or god, I say, and still appeareth not?
What is his name?   What rank and guise hath he,
Whom winds and spirits serve, who honoureth thee
Above all others in thy blifsful lot?"

10.

But Psyche when that wistful speech she heard
Was ware of all her spouse had warned her of :
And uttering a disingenuous word,
Said " A youth yet unbearded is my love.
He goeth hunting on the plains to-day,
And with his dogs hath wandered far away ;
And not till eve can he return above."

11.

Then fearing to be nearer plied, she rose
And brought her richest jewels one by one,
Bidding them choose and take whate'er they chose ;
And beckoning the Zephyr spake anon
That he should waft her sisters to the peak ;
The which he did, and, ere they more could speak,
They rose on high, and in the wind were gone.

12.

Nor till again they came upon the road,
Which from the mountain shoulder o'er the plain
Led to the city of their sire's abode,

Found they their tongues, though full of high disdain
Their hearts were, but kept silence, till the strength
Of pride and envious hatred burst at length
In speech, and thus the elder gan complain :

13.

" Cruel and unjust fortune ! that of three
Sisters, whose being from one fountain welled
Exalts the last so high from her degree,
And leaves the first to be so far excelled.
My husband is a poor and niggard churl
To him, whoe'er he be, that loves the girl.
Oh ! in what godlike state her house is held !"

14.

" Ay," said the other, " to a gouty loon
Am I not wedded ?   See thy hurt is mine.
But never call me woman more, if soon
I cannot lure her from her height divine.
Nay, she shall need her cunning wit to save
The wealth of which so grudgingly she gave ;
Wherefore thy hand and heart with me combine.

15.

" She but received us out of pride, to show
Her state, well deeming that her happinefs
Was little worth while there was none to know;
So is our lot uninjured if none guefs.
Reveal we nothing therefore, but the while
Together scheme this wanton to beguile,
And bring her boasting godhead to distrefs."

16.

So fresh disordering their drefs and hair,
With loud lament they to their sire return,
Telling they found not Psyche anywhere,
And of her sure mischance could nothing learn.
Whereat he sank apace ; but they had shent
Their piety, and straightway home they went,
Nor longer let his grief their hearts concern.

17.

Meanwhile her unknown lover did not cease
To warn poor Psyche how her sisters planned
To undermine her love and joy and peace :

And urged how well she might their wiles withstand,
By keeping them from her delight aloof:
For better is security than proof,
And malice held afar than near at hand.

18.

" And, dearest wife " he said, " since 'tis not long
Ere one will come to share thy secresy,
And be thy babe and mine; let nothing wrong
The happy months of thy maternity.
If thou keep trust, then shalt thou see thy child
A god; but if to pry thou be beguiled,
The lot of both is death and misery."

19.

Then Psyche's simple heart was filled with joy,
And counting up the months and hours and days,
Looked for the time, when she should bear a boy
To be her growing stay and godlike praise.
And " O be sure " she said, " be sure, my pride
Having so rich a promise cannot slide,
Even though my love could fail which thee obeys."

20.

And so most happily her life went by,
In thoughts of love dear to her new estate;
Until at length the evil day drew nigh,
When now her sisters, joined in jealous hate,
Together were set forth upon their way,
Plotting how best to make her speech betray
Her secret, and how lure her by what bait.

21.

That night her husband spake to her, and said
" Psyche, thy sisters come : and when they climb
The peak they will not tarry to be sped
Down by the Zephyr, as that other time,
But fond in confidence will cast themselves
Into the air, and on the rocky shelves
Be dashed, and pay the penalty of crime.

22.

" So let it be, and so shall we be saved."
Which meditated vengeance of his fear
When Psyche heard, now for their life she craved,

Whose mere distrefs erewhile had touched her near
Around her lover's neck her arms she threw,
And pleaded for them by her faith so true,
Although they went on doom in judgment clear.

23.

In terror of bloodguiltinefs she now
Forgot all other danger, she adjured,
Or using playfulnefs deep sobs would plow
Her soft entreaties, not to be endured;
Till he at last was fain once more to grant
The service of the Zephyr to enchant
That wicked couple from their fate afsured.

24.

So ere 'twas noon were noises at the door
Of knocking loud and voices high in glee;
Such as within that vale never before
Had been, and now seemed most unmeet to be.
And Pysche blushed, though being alone, and rose
To meet her sisters and herself unclose
The gate that made them of her palace free.

E

25.

Fondly she kiſsed them, and with kindly cheer
Sought to amuse; and they with outward smile
O'ermasked their hate, and called her sweet and dear,
Finding affection easy to beguile:
And all was smooth, until at last one said
" Tell us, I pray, to whom 'tis thou art wed;
Mong gods or men, what is his rank and style?

26.

" Thou canst not think to hide the truth from us,
Who knew thy peevish sorrows when a maid,
And see thee now so glad and rapturous,
As changed from what thou wert as light from shade;
Thy jewels too, the palace of a king,
Nor least the serviceable spiriting,
By all these things thy secret is betrayed :

27.

" And yet thou talkest of thy wondrous man
No more than if his face thou didst not know."
At which incontinently she began,

Forgetful of her words a month ago,
Answering " A merchant rich, of middle age,
My husband is ; and o'er his features sage
His temples are already touched with snow.

28.

"But 'gainst his wish since hither ye were brought
'Twere best depart."   Then her accustomed spell
Sped them upon the summit quick as thought ;
And being alone her doing pleased her well :
So was she vexed to find her love at night
More sad than ever, of her sisters' spite
Speaking as one that could the end foretell.

29.

" To-morrow " said he " will they spy again,
Let them be dashed upon the rocks and die ;
'Tis they must come to death or thou to pain,
To separation, Psyche, thou and I ;
Nay, and our babe to ill.   I therefore crave
Thou wilt not even once more these vipers save,
Nor to thy love his only boon deny."

30.

But Psyche would not think her sisters' crime
So grofs and strange, nor could her danger see;
Since 'twere so easy if at any time
They showed the venom of their hearts, that she
Should fan them off upon the willing gust.
So she refused, and claiming truer trust
Would in no wise unto their death agree.

MEASURE V.

1.

"WHAT think you, sister:" thus one envious fiend
To other spake upon their homeward route,
"What think you of the knowledge we have gleaned
Of this mysterious lover, who can shoot
In thirty days from beardlefs youth to prime,
With wisdom in his face before his time,
And snowy locks upon his head to boot?"

2.

"Ay," said the other, "true, she lied not well;
And thence I gather knows no more than we:
For surely 'tis a spirit insensible
To whom she is wedded, one she cannot see.
'Tis that I fear; for if 'tis so, her child
Will be a god, and she a goddefs styled,
Which, though I die to let it, shall not be.

3.

"Lament we thus no longer.　Come, consult
What may be done."　And home they came at night,
Yet not to rest, but of their plots occult
Sat whispering on their beds ; and ere 'twas light
Resolved, but could not so the deed defer,
But roused the house ere dawn with sudden stir
And sallied forth in haste to work their spite.

4.

And with the day were climbed upon the peak,
And swam down on the Zephyr as before ;
But now with piercing cry and doleful shriek
They force their entrance through the golden door,
Feigning the urgency of bitter truth ;
Such as deforms a friendly face with ruth,
When kindnefs may not hide ill tidings more.

5.

Then Psyche when she heard their wailful din,
And saw their countenances wan and worn
With travel, vigil, and disfiguring sin,

Their hair dishevelled and their habits torn,
For trembling scarce could ask what ill had happed;
And they alert with joy to see her trapped,
Launched forth amain, and on their drift were borne.

6.

"O Psyche, happiest certainly and blest
Up to this hour" they said "thou surely wert,
Being of thy fearful peril unpofsefsed,
Which now we would not tell but to avert.
But we for firm and solemn truth have found
Thy spouse to be a dragon wide-renowned,
Who holds thee here to work thy shame and hurt.

7.

" As yesternight we rode upon the wind
He ifsued to pursue us from the wood;
We saw his back, that through the tree-tops finned,
His fiery eyes glared from their wrinkled hood.
Lo, now betimes the oracle, which said
How to the savage beast thou should'st be wed,
Is plainly for thy safety understood.

8.

" Long time hath he been known to all that dwell
Upon the plain; but now his secret lair
Have we discovered, which none else could tell:
Though many women fallen in his snare
Hath he enchanted; who, tradition saith,
Taste love awhile, ere to their cruel death
They paſs in turn upon the summits bare.

9.

" Fly with us while thou mayst : no more delay;
Renounce the spells of this accursed vale.
We come to save thee, but we dare not stay ;
Among these sightleſs spirits our senses quail.
Fly with us, fly ! " Then Psyche, for her soul
Was soft and simple, lost her self control,
And, thinking only of the horrid tale,

10.

" Dear Sisters " said she, and her sobbing speech
Was broken by her terror, " it is true
That much hath happed to stablish what ye teach;

For ne'er hath it been granted me to view
My husband; and, for aught I know, he may
Be even that cruel dragon, which ye say
Sprang on you from the forest to pursue.

11.

"'Tis sure that scarcely can I win his grace
To see you here; and still he mischief vows
If ever I should ask to see his face,
Which, coming in the dark, he ne'er allows.
Therefore, if ye can help, of pity show,
Since doubt I must, how I may come to know
What kind of spirit it is that is my spouse."

12.

Then to her cue the younger was afore:
" Hide thou a razor " cried she " near thy bed;
And have a lamp prepared, but whelm thereo'er
Some cover, that no light be from it shed.
And when securely in first sleep he lies,
Look on him well, and ere he can arise,
Gashing his throat, cut off his hideous head."

13.

Which both persuading, off they flew content,
Divining that the thing she was forbid
Was by her lover for her safety meant,
Which only could be sure while he was hid.
But Psyche, to that miserable deed
Being now already in her mind agreed,
Wandered alone, and knew not what she did.

14.

Now she would trust her lover, now in turn
Made question of his bidding as unjust;
Nor could it do him injury to learn
That he was not that monster of disgust
Whose horrid cruelty her heart had scared.
But fear at length o'ercame; and she prepared
The mean contrivance of her blind mistrust.

15.

She set the lamp beneath a chair, and cloked
Thickly its rebel lustre from the eye:
And laid the knife, to mortal keennefs stroked,

Within her reach, near where she wont to lie:
And took her place full early; but her heart
Beat fast, and stayed her breath with sudden start,
Feeling her lover's arm laid fond thereby.

16.

But when at last he slept, then she arose,
All faint and tremulous: and though it be
That wrong to such sheer innocence hath shews
Of novelty, its guilt from shame to free,
Yet 'twas for shame her hand so strangely shook
That held the steel, and from the cloke that took
The lamp, and raised it o'er the bed to see.

17.

She had some fear she might not well discern
By that small flame a monster in the gloom,
When lo! the air about her seemed to burn,
And bright celestial radiance filled the room.
Too plainly O she saw, O fair to see!
Eros, 'twas Eros' self, her lover, he
The God of love, revealed in deathlefs bloom.

18.

Her fainting strength forsook her; on her knees
Down by the bed she sank; the shamelefs knife
Fell flashing, and her heart took thought to seize
Its desperate haft, and end her wicked life.
Yet not could she her amorous eyes withdraw
From off her lover, now whom first she saw
Only to know she was no more his wife.

19.

O treasure of all treasures, late her own!
O lofs above all lofses, lost for aye!
Since there was no repentance could atone
For her dishonour, nor her fate withstay.
But yet 'twas joy to have her love in sight;
And, yielding to the rapture while she might,
She gazed upon his body where he lay.

20.

Above all mortal beauty, as was hers,
She saw a rival; but if pafsion's heart
Be rightly read by subtle questioners,

Measure V.

It owns a wanton and a gentler part.
And Psyche smiled, noting each outward sign
By which the immortal God, her spouse divine,
Confeſsed the type which blinds our earthlier art

21.

His thickly curling hair, his ruddy cheeks,
And pouting lips, his soft and dimpled chin,
The full and cushioned eye, that ever speaks
Of self-content and thoughtleſsneſs within,
The forward, froward ear, and smooth to touch
His body sleek, but rounded overmuch
For dignity of mind and pride akin.

22.

She noted that the small irradiant wings,
That down his shoulders lay spread out at rest,
Were yet disturbed with gentle quiverings,
As if some wakeful spirit his blood poſsest,
She feared he was awaking, but they kept
Their sweet commotion still, and still he slept,
And still she gazed with never-tiring zest.

23.

And now the colour of her pride and joy
Outflushed the hue of Eros; she, so cold,
To have fired the pafsion of the heartlefs boy,
Whom none in heaven or earth were found to hold!
Psyche, the earthborn, to be prized above
The heavenly Graces by the God of love,
And worshipped by his wantonnefs untold!

24.

Nay, for that very thing she loved him more,
More than herself her sweet self's complement:
Until the sight of him again upbore
Her courage, and renewed her vigour spent.
And looking now around, she first espied
Where at the bed's foot, cast in haste aside,
Lay his full quiver, and his bow unbent.

25.

One of those darts, of which she had heard so oft,
She took to try if 'twas so very keen;
And held its point against her finger soft

So gently, that to touch it scarce was seen ;
Yet was she sharply pricked, and felt the fire
Run through her veins ; and now a strange desire
Troubled her heart, which ne'er before had been :

26.

Straight sprang she to her lover on the bed,
And kifsed his cheek, and was not satisfied :
When, oh ! the lamp, held ill-balanced o'erhead,
One drop of burning oil spilled from its side
On Eros' naked shoulder as he slept,
Who wakened by the sudden smart upleapt
Upon the floor, and all the mischief eyed.

27.

With nervous speed he seized his bow, and pafsed
Out of the guilty chamber at a bound ;
But Psyche, following his flight as fast,
Caught him, and crying threw her arms around.
Till coming to the court he rose in air ;
And she, close clinging in her last despair,
Was dragged, and then lost hold and fell to ground.

28.

Wailing she fell ; but he, upon the roof
Staying his feet, awhile his flight delayed :
And turning to her as he stood aloof
Beside a cyprefs, whose profoundest shade
Drank the reflections of the dreamy night
In its stiff pinnacle, the nimble light
Of million stars upon his body played.

29.

" O simple-hearted Psyche," thus he spake,
And she upraised her piteous eyes and hands,
" O simple-hearted Psyche, for thy sake
Dared I to break my mother's stern commands ;
And gave thee godlike marriage in the place
Of vilest shame ; and, not to hurt thy grace,
Spared thee my arrows, which no heart withstands.

30.

" But thou, for doubt I was some evil beast,
Hast mocked the warning of my love, to spy
Upon my secrets, which concerned thee least,

Seeing that thy joy was never touched thereby.
By faithlefs prying thou hast worked thy fall,
And, even as I foretold thee, losest all
For looking on thy happinefs too nigh.

31.

" Which lofs may be thine ample punishment.
But to those fiends, by whom thou wert misled,
Go tell each one in turn that I have sent
This mefsage, that I love her in thy stead;
And bid them by their love haste hither soon."
Whereat he fled ; and Psyche in a swoon
Fell back upon the marble floor as dead.

F

MEASURE VI.

1.

WHEN from the lowest ebbings of her blood
  The fluttering pulses thrilled and swelled
    again,
Her stricken heart recovering force to flood
With life the sunken conduits of her brain,
Then Psyche, where she had fallen, numb and-cold
Arose, but scarce her quaking sense controlled,
Seeing the couch where she that night had lain.

2.

The level sunbeams searched the grassy ground
For diamond dewdrops.   Ah ! was this the place ?
Where was the court, her home ? She looked around

And questioned with her memory for a space.
There was the cyprefs, there the well-known wood,
That walled the spot : 'twas here her palace stood,
As surely as 'twas vanished without trace.

3.

Was all a dream ?   To think that all was dreamt
Were now the happier thought ; but arguing o'er
That dream it was, she fell from her attempt,
Feeling the wifely burden that she bore.
Nay, true, 'twas true.   She had had all and lost ;
The joy, the recklefs wrong, the heavy cost
Were hers, the dead end now, and woe in store.

4.

What to be done ? Fainting and shelterlefs
Among the mountains was no place to bide :
And harbour knew she none, where her distrefs
Might comfort find, or love's dishonour hide ;
Nor now felt any dread like that of home :
Yet forth she must, albeit to rove and roam
An outcast o'er the country far and wide.

5.

Anon she marvelled noting from the vale
A path lead downward to the plain below,
Crofsing the very site, whereon the pale
Of all her joy had stood few hours ago ;
A run of mountain beasts, that keep their track
Through generations, and for ages back
Had trod the self-same footing to and fro.

6.

That would she try : so forth she took her way,
Turning her face from the dishonoured dell,
Adown the broadening eastward lawns, which lay
In gentle slant, till suddenly they fell
In sheer cliff ; whence the path that went around,
Clomb by the bluffs or e'er it downward wound
Beneath that precipice impafsable.

7.

There once she turned, and gazing up the slope
She bid the scene of all her joys adieu ;
" Ay, and farewell " she cried, " farewell to hope,

Since there is none will rescue me anew,
Who have killed God's perfection with a doubt."
Which said, she took the path that led about,
And hid the upland pleasance from her view.

8.

But soon it left her, entering neath the shades
Of cedar old and rufseted tall pine,
Whose mighty tops, seen from the thorny glades
Belted the hills about ; and now no sign
Had she to guide her, save the slow descent.
But swiftly o'er the springy floor she went,
And drew the odorous air like draughts of wine.

9.

Then next she pafsed a forest thick and dark
With heavy ilexes and platanes high,
And came to long lush grafs ; and now could mark
By many a token that the plain was nigh.
When, lo ! a river : to whose brink at last
Being come, upon the bank her limbs she cast,
And through her sad tears watched the stream go by.

10.

And now the thought came o'er her that in death
There was a cure for sorrow, that before
Her eyes ran Lethe, she might take one breath
Of water and be freed for evermore.
Leaning to look into her tomb, thereon
She saw the horror of her image wan,
And up she rose at height to leap from shore.

11.

When suddenly a mighty voice, that fell
With fury on her ears, their sense to scare,
That bounding from the tree trunks like the yell
Of hundred brazen trumpets, cried " Forbear !
Forbear, fond maid, that froward step to take,
For life can cure the ills that love may make ;
But for the harm of death is no repair."

12.

Then looking up she saw an uncouth form
Perched on the further bank, whose parted lips
Volleyed their friendly warning in a storm:

A man he might have been, but for the tips
Of horns appearing from his shaggy head;
For o'er his matted beard his face was red,
And all his shape was manlike to the hips.

13.

In forehead low, keen eye, and nostril flat
He bore the human grace in mean degree,
But, set beneath his body squat and fat,
Legs like a goat's, and from the hairy knee
The shank fell spare; and, though crofswise he put
His limbs in easeful posture, for the foot
The beast's divided hoof was plain to see.

14.

Him then she knew the mighty choric God,
The great hill-haunting and tree-loving Pan;
Whom Zeus had laughed to see when first he trod
Olympus, neither god nor beast nor man :
Who every rocky peak and snow-capped crest
Of the Aspran mountains for his own pofsest,
And all their wastes with bacchic rout o'erran.

15.

Whom, when his pipe he plays on loud and sweet,
And o'er the fitted reeds his moist lip flees,
Around in measured step with nimble feet
Dance water-nymphs and Hamadryades:
And all the woodland's airy folk, who shun
Man's presence, to his frolic pastime run
From their perennial wells and sacred trees.

16.

Now on his knee his pipe laid by, he spoke
With flippant tongue, wounding unwittingly
The heart he sought to cheer with jest and joke.
" And what hast thou to do with misery "
He said, " who hast such beauty as might gain
The love of Eros? Cast away thy pain,
And give thy soul to mirth and jollity.

17.

" Thy mortal life is but a brittle vase,
But as thee list with wine or tears 'tis filled;
For all the drops therein are Ohs and Ahs

Of woe or pleasure as thy wit hath willed ;
And shouldst thou learn of me my merry way,
I'd teach thee change thy lover every day,
And prize the precious cup thou wouldst have spilled.

18.

" Nay, if thou plunge thou shalt not drown nor sink,
For I will to thee o'er the stream afloat,
And bear thee safe ; and oh ! I know a drink
For care, that makes sweet music in the throat.
Come live with me, my love ; I'll cure thy chance :
For I can laugh and quaff, and pipe and dance,
Swim like a fish, and caper like a goat."

19.

Speaking, his brute divinity explored
The secret of her silence ; and old Pan
In kindnefs told her of a shallow ford
Where lower down the stream o'er pebbles ran,
And one might pafs at ease with ankles dry :
Whither she went, and crofsing o'er thereby,
Her lonely wanderings through the isle began.

20.

But none could tell, no, nor herself had told
Where food she found, or shelter through the land
By day or night ; until by fate controlled
She came by steep ways to the southern strand,
Where, sacred to the Twins and Britomart,
Pent in its rocky theatre apart,
A little town stood on the level sand.

21.

'Twas where her younger sister's husband reigned :
And Psyche to the palace gate drew near,
Helplefsly still by Eros' hest constrained,
And knocking begged to see her sister dear ;
But when in state stepped down that haughty queen,
And saw the wan face spent with tears and teen,
She smiled, and said "Psyche, what dost thou here?"

22.

Then Psyche told how, having well employed
Their means, and done their bidding not amifs,
Looking on him her hand would have destroyed,

'Twas Eros; whom in love leaning to kiſs,
Even as she kiſsed, a drop of burning oil
Fall'n from the lamp had served her scheme to foil
Discovering her in vision of her bliſs;

23.

Wherewith the god stung, like a startled bird
Arose in air, and she fell back in swoon ;
" But ere he parted " said she, " he conferred
On thee the irrecoverable boon
My prying lost to me : *Go tell* he said
Thy sister that I love her in thy stead,
And bid her by her love haste hither soon."

24.

Which when that heart of malice heard, it took
The jealous fancy of her silly lust :
And pitileſsly with triumphant look
She drank the flattery, and gave full trust ;
And leaving Psyche ere she more could tell,
Ran off to bid her spouse for aye farewell,
And in his ear this ready lie she thrust :

25.

" My dearest sister Psyche, she whose fate
We mourned, hath reappeared alive and hale,
But brings sad news ; my father dies : full late
These tidings come, but love may yet avail ;
Let me be gone." And stealing blind consent,
Forth on that well-remembered road she went,
And climbed upon the peak above the dale.

26.

There on the topmost rocks, where Psyche first
Had by her weeping sire been left to die,
She stood a moment, in her hope accurst
Being happy ; and the cliffs took up her cry
With chuckling mockery from her tongue above,
Zephyr, sweet Zephyr, waft me to my love !
When off she leapt upon his wings to fly.

27.

But as a dead stone, from a height let fall,
Silent and straight is gathered by the force
Of earth's vast mafs upon its weight so small,

In speed increasing as it nears its source
Of motion—by which law all things soe'er
Are clutched and dragged and held—so fell she there,
Like a dead stone, down, in her headlong course.

28.

The disregardful silence heard her strike
Upon the solid crags ; her dismal shriek
Rang on the rocks and died out laughter-like
Along the vale in hurried trebles weak ;
And soon upon her, from their skiey haunt
Fell to their feast the great birds bald and gaunt,
And gorged on her fair flesh with bloody beak.

29.

But Psyche, when her sister was gone forth,
Went out again her wandering way to take :
And following a stream that led her north,
After some days she pafsed the Corian Lake,
Whereby Athena's temple stands, and he
Who traverses the isle from sea to sea
May by the plain his shortest journey make.

30.

Till on the northern coast arrived she came
Upon a city built about a port,
The which she knew, soon as she heard the name,
Was where her eldest sister held her court;
To whom, as Eros had commanded her,
She now in turn became the mefsenger   .
Of vengeful punishment, that fell not short.

31.

For she too hearing gan her heart exalt,
Nor pity felt for Psyche's tears and moans,
But, fellowed with that other in her fault,
Followed her to her fate upon the stones;
And from the peak leaping like her below
The self-same way unto the self-same woe,
Lay dashed to death upon her sister's bones.

MEASURE VII.

I.

BESIDE the Hellenic board of Crete's fair
       isle,
  Westward of Drepanon, along a reach
Which maſsy Cyamum for many a mile
Jutting to sea delivers from the breach
Of North and East,—returning to embay
The favoured shore—an ancient city lay,
Aptera, which is *Wingleſs* in our speech.

2.

And hence the name ; that here in rocky cove,
Thence called Museion, was the contest waged
What day the Sirens with the Muses strove,
By jealous Hera in that war engaged :
Wherein the daughters of Mnemosynè
O'ercame the chauntreſses who vexed the sea,
Nor vengeance spared them by their pride enraged.

3.

For those strange creatures, who with women's words
And wiles made ravenous prey of paſsers-by,
Were throated with the liquid pipe of birds :
Of love they sang ; and none, who sailed anigh
Through the grey hazes of the cyanine sea,
Had wit the whirlpool of that song to flee,
Nor feared the talon hooked and feathered thigh.

4.

But them the singers of the gods o'ercame,
And plucked them of their plumage, where in fright
They flew to scape their punishment and shame,
Upon two rocks that lie within the bight,
Under the headland, barren and alone ;
Which, being with the scattered feathers strewn,
Were by the folk named Leukæ, which is *White.*

5.

Thereon about this time the snowy gull,
Minion of Aphrodite, being come,
Plumed himself, standing on the sea-wrack dull,

That drifted from the foot of Cyamum;
And 'twas his thought, that had the goddefs learnt
The tale of Psyche loved and Eros burnt,
She ne'er so long had kept aloof and dumb.

6.

Wherefore that duteous gofsip of Love's queen
Devised that he the mefsenger would be;
And rising from the rock, he skimmed between
The chasing waves—such grace have none but he;—
Into the middle deep then down he dived,
And rowing with his glistening wings, arrived
At Aphrodite's bower beneath the sea.

7.

The eddies from his silver pinions swirled
The crimson, green, and yellow flofs, that grew
About the caves, and at his pafsing curled
Its graceful silk, and gently waved anew:
Till, oaring here and there, the queen he found
Strayed from her haunt unto a sandy ground,
Dappled with eye-rings in the sunlight blue.

G

8.

She, as he came upon her from above,
With Hora played; Hora, her herald fair,
That lays the soft necefsity of Love
On maidens' eyelids, and with sweetest care
Marketh the hour, as in all works is fit;
And happy they in love who time outwit,
Fondly constrainèd in her season rare.

9.

But he with garrulous and laughing tongue
Broke up his news; how Eros, fallen sick,
Lay tofsing on his bed, to frenzy stung
By such a burn as did but barely prick:
A little bleb, no bigger than a pease,
Upon his shoulder 'twas, that killed his ease,
Fevered his heart, and made his breathing thick.

10.

" For which disaster hath he not been seen
This many a day at all in any place:
And thou, dear mistrefs," said he " hast not been

Thyself amongst us now a dreary space :
And pining mortals suffer from a dearth
Of love; and for this sadnefs of the earth
Thy family is darkened with disgrace.

11.

" Now on the secret paths of dale and wood,
Where lovers walked, lovers are none to find :
And friends, besworn to closest brotherhood,
Forget their faith, and part with words unkind :
By latest married folk thy bond is loathed :
And I could tell even of the new-betrothed
That fly o'erseas, and leave their loves behind.

12.

"Summer is over, but the merry pipe,
That wont to cheer the harvesting, is mute :
And in the vineyards, where the grape is ripe,
No voice is heard of them that take the fruit.
No workman sings at eve nor maidens dance :
All joy is dead, and with the year's advance
The signs of woe increase on man and brute.

13.

" 'Tis plain that if thy pleasure longer pause
Thy mighty rule on earth has seen its day :
The race must come to perish, and no cause
But that thou sittest with thy nymphs at play,
While on the Cretan hills thy truant boy
Has with his pretty mistrefs turned to toy,
And lefs for pain than love now pines away."

14.

" Ha! Mistrefs!" cried she ; " Hath my beardlefs son
Been hunting for himself his lovely game ?
Some young Orestiad hath his fancy won ?
Some Naiad ? say; or is a Grace his flame ?
Or maybe Muse, and then 'tis Erato ;
She aye was wanton.   Tell, if thou dost know,
Woman or goddefs is she ? and her name."

15.

Then said the snowy gull " O heavenly queen,
What is my knowledge, who am but a bird ?
Yet is she only mortal, as I ween,

And namèd Psyche, if I rightly heard."—
But Aphrodite's look daunted his cheer,
Screaming he fled away, scared even by fear
To see the wrath his simple tale had stirred.

16.

He flashed his pens, and sweeping widely round
Towered to air; so swift in all his way,
That whence he dived he there again was found
As soon as if he had but dipped for prey :
And now, or e'er he joined his sacred flock,
Once more he stood upon the Sirens' rock,
And pruned his ruffled quills for fresh display.

17.

But as ill tidings have their truth afsured
Without more witnefs than their fatal sense,
So, since was nought she lefs could have endured,
The injured goddefs guefsed the full offence :
And doubted only whether first to smite
Or Psyche for her new presumptuous flight,
Or Eros for his disobedience.

18.

But full of anger to her son she went,
And found him in his golden chamber laid,
And with him sweet Euphrosynè, attent
Upon his murmured wants, aye as he bade
Shifted the pillows with each fretful whim;
But scornfully his mother looked at him,
And recklefs of his pain gan thus upbraid:

19.

"O worthy deeds, I say, and true to blood,
The crown and pledge of promise! thou that wast
In estimation my perpetual bud,
Now fruiting thus untimely to my cost;
Backsliding from commandment, ay, and worse,
With blifs to favour one I bade thee curse,
And save the life I left with thee for lost!

20.

" Thou too to burn with love, and love of her
Whom I did hate; and to thy bed to take
My rival, that my trusted officer

Might of mine enemy my daughter make!
Dost thou then think my love for thee so fond,
And miserably doting, that the bond
By such dishonour strainèd will not break?

21.

" Or that I cannot bear another son
As good as thou; or, if I choose not bear,
Not beg a lusty boy of any one
Of all my nymphs,—and some have boys to spare,—
One I might train, to whom thine arms made o'er
Should do me kinder service than before,
To smite my foes and keep my honour fair?

22.

" For thou hast ever mocked me, and beguiled
In amours strange my God thy valiant sire:
And having smirched our fame while yet a child,
Wilt further foul it now with earthly fire.
But I—do as thou mayst—have vowed to kill
Thy fancied girl, whether thou love her still,
Or of her silly charms already tire.

23.

"Tell me but where she hides." And Eros now,
Proud in his woe, boasted his happy theft:
Confeſsing he had loved her well, and how
By her own doing she was lost and left;
And homeleſs in such sorrow as outwent
The utmost pains of other punishment,
Was wandering of his love and favour reft.

24.

By which was Cypris gladdened, not appeased,
But hid her joy and spake no more her threat:
And left with face like one that much displeased
First bending deigns a sign he may forget.
When lo! as swiftly she came stepping down
From her fair house into the heavenly town,
The Kronian sisters on the way she met.

25.

Hera the Wife of Zeus, her placid front
Dark with the shadow of his troubled reign,
And tall Demeter, who with men once wont,

Holding the high Olympians in disdain
For Persephafsa's rape; which now forgiven,
She was returned unto the courts of Heaven,
And 'mong the immortals lived at peace again.

26.

Whose smile told Aphrodite that they knew
The meaning of her visit; and a flush
Of anger answered them, while hot she grew.
But Hera laughed outright: "Why thou dost blush!
Now see we modest manners on my life!
And all thy little son has got a wife
Can make the crimson to thy forehead rush.

27.

"Didst think he, whom thou madest pafsion's prince,
No privy dart then for himself would poise?
Nay, by the cuckoo on my sceptre, since
'Twas love made thee the mother of his joys,
Art thou the foremost to his favour bound;
As thou shouldst be the last to think to sound
The heart, and least of all thy wanton boy's."

28.

But her Demeter, on whose stalwart arm
She leaned, took up : " If thou wilt list to me,
This Psyche " said she " hath the heavenly charm,
And will become immortal.   And maybe
To marry with a woman is as well
As wed a god and live below in Hell :
As 'twas my lot in child of mine to see."

29.

Which things they both said, fearing in their hearts
That savage Eros, if they mocked his case,
Would kill their peace with his revengeful darts,
And bring them haply to a worse disgrace :
But Aphrodite, saying " Good ! my dames ;
Behind this smoke I see the spite that flames,"
Left them, and on her journey went apace.

30.

For having purposed she would hold no truce
With Psyche or her son, 'twas in her mind
To go forthwith unto the house of Zeus,

And beg that Hermes might be sent to find
The wanderer; and secure that in such quest
He would not fail, she pondered but how best
She might inflict the vengeance she designed.

MEASURE VIII.

I.

HEAVY meanwhile at heart, with bruisèd
    feet
  Was Psyche wandering many nights and
    days
Upon the paths of hundred-citied Crete,
And chose to step the most deserted ways;
Being least unhappy when she went unseen;
Since else her secret sorrow had no screen
From the plain question of men's idle gaze.

2.

Yet wheresoe'er she went one hope she had;
Like mortal mourners, who 'gainst reason strong
Hope to be unexpectedly made glad

With sight of their dead friends, so much they long;
So she for him, whom lofs a thousandfold
Endeared and made desired ; nor could she hold
He would not turn and quite forgive her wrong.

3.

Wherefore her eager eyes in every place
Looked for her lover; and 'twixt hope and fear
She followed off afar some form of grace,
In pain alike to lose or venture near.
And still this thought cheered her fatigue, that he,
Or on some hill, or by some brook or tree,
But waited for her coming to appear.

4.

And then for comfort many an old love-crofsed
And doleful ditty would she gently sing,
Writ by sad poets of a lover lost,
Now sounding sweeter for her sorrowing :
Echo, sweet Echo, watching up on high,
Say hast thou seen to-day my love go by,
Or where thou sittest by thy mofsy spring?

5.

Or say ye nymphs, that from the crystal rills,
When ye have bathed y.our limbs from morn till eve,
Flying at midnight to the bare-topped hills,
Beneath the stars your mazy dances weave,
Say, my deserter, whom ye well may know
By his small wings, his quiver, and his bow,
Say, have ye seen my love, whose lofs I grieve?

6.

Till climbed one evening on a rocky steep
Above the plain of Cisamos, that lay,
Robbed of its golden harvest, in the deep
Mountainous shadows of the dying day,
She saw a temple, whose tall columns fair
Recalled her home; and "O if thou be there,
My love," she cried, " fly not again away."

7.

Swiftly she ran, and entering by the door
She stood alone within an empty fane
Of great Demeter : and, behold ! the floor

Was thickly strewn about with scattered grain,
And ears of wheat and bearded barley heaped,
The first fruits thither borne of them that reaped
The goddefs' plenteous gifts upon the plain,

8.

And on the tithe the tackle of the tithe
Thrown by in such confusion, as are laid
Upon the swath sickle, and hook, and scythe,
When midday drives the reapers to the shade.
And Psyche, since had come no priestefs there
To trim the temple, in her pious care
Forgat herself, and lent her duteous aid.

9.

She drew the offerings from the midst aside,
And piled the stooks at every pillar's base;
And sweeping therebetween a pafsage wide,
Made clear of corn and chaff the temple space :
Even as when countrymen bring wheat to mart,
They set their show along the walls apart
By their allotted stations, each in place,

10.

Thus she, and felt no wearinefs;—such strength
Hath duty to support our feeble frame;—
Till all was set in order, and at length
Up to the threshold of the Shrine she came:
When lo! before her face with friendly smile,
Tall as a pillar of the periſtyle,
The goddefs stood revealed, and called her name.

11.

" Unhappy Psyche," said she, " knowst thou not
How Aphrodite to thy hurt is sworn?
And thou, thy peril and her wrath forgot,
Spendest thy thought my temple to adorn.
Take better heed!"—And Psyche, at the voice
Even of so little comfort, gan rejoice,
And at her feet poured out this prayer forlorn.

12.

" O Gracious giver of the golden grain,
Hide me, I pray thee, from her wrath unkind;
For who can pity, as canst thou my pain,

Who wert thyself a wanderer, vexed in mind
For lofs of thy sweet Corè once, whenas,
Ravished to hell by fierce Agesilas,
Thou soughtest her on earth and couldst not find.

13.

" How could thy feet bear thee to western night,
And where swart Libyans watch the sacred tree,
And thrice to ford o'er Achelous bright,
And all the streams of beauteous Sicily?
And thrice to Enna cam'st thou, thrice, they tell,
Satest by Callichorus' sacred well,
Nor tookest of its spring to comfort thee.

14.

" By that remembered anguish of thine heart,
Lady, have pity even on me, and show
Where I may find my love ; and take my part
For peace, beseech thee, 'gainst my cruel foe :
Or if thou canst not from her anger shield,
Here let me lie among the sheaves concealed
Such time till forth I may in safety go."

H

15.

Demeter answered "Nay, though thou constrain'st
My favour with thy plea, my help must still
Be secret, for I may not move against
A sister goddefs, whatsoe'er her will.
Thou must fly hence :   Yet though I not oppose,
Less will I aid her ; and if now I close
My temple doors to thee, take it not ill."

16.

Then Psyche's hope foundered ; as when a ship,
The morrow of the tempest, scarcely rides
The swollen seas, fetching a deeper dip
At every wave, and through her gaping sides
And o'er her shattered bulwarks ever drinks,
Till plunging in the watery toils she sinks,
To swim all undersea the sightlefs tides :

17.

So with each word her broken spirit drank
Its doom ; and overwhelmed with deep despair
She turned away, and coming forth she sank

Silently weeping on the temple stair,
In midmost night, forspent with long turmoil :
But sleep, the gracious pursuivant of toil,
Came swiftly down, and nursed away her care.

18.

And when the sun awaked her with his beams
She found new hope, that still her sorrow's cure
Lay with the gods, who in her morning dreams
Had sent her comfort in a vision sure ;
Wherein the Cretan-born, almightiest god,
Cloud-gathering Zeus himself had seemed to nod,
And bid her with good heart her woes endure.

19.

So coming that same day unto a shrine
Of Hera, she took courage and went in :
And like to one that to the cell divine
For favour ventures or a suit to win,
She drew anigh the altar, from her face
Wiping the tears, ere to the heavenly grace,
As thus she prayed, she would her prayer begin.

20.

" Most honoured Lady, who from ancient doom
Wert made heaven's wife, and art on earth besought
With gracious happinefs of all to whom
Thy sacred wedlock hath my burden brought,
Save me from Aphrodite's fell pursuit,
And guard unto the birth Love's haplefs fruit,
Which she for cruel spite would bring to nought.

21.

" As once from her thou wert not shamed to take
Her beauty's zone, thy beauty to enhance;
For which again Zeus loved thee, to forsake
His warlike ire in faithful dalliance ;
Show me what means may win my Love to me,
Or how that I may come, if so may be,
Within the favour of his countenance.

22.

" If there be any place for tears or prayer,
If there be need for succour in distrefs,
Now is the very hour of all despair,

Here is the heart of grief and bitternefs.
Motherly pity, bend thy face and grant
One beam of ruth to thy poor suppliant,
Nor turn me from thine altar comfortlefs."

23.

Even as she prayed a cloud spread through the cell
And mid the wreathings of the vapour dim
The goddefs grew in glory visible,
Like some barbaric queen in festal trim ;
Such the attire and ornaments she wore,
When o'er the forgèd threshold of the floor
Of Zeus's house she stepped to visit him.

24.

From either ear, ringed to its piercèd lobe
A triple jewel hung, with gold enchased ;
And o'er her breasts her wide ambrosial robe
With many a shining golden clasp was braced ;
The flowering on its smooth embroidered lawn
Gathered to colour where the zone was drawn
In fringe of golden tafsels at her waist.

25.

Her curling hair with plaited braid and brail,
Pendant or looped about her head divine,
Lay hidden half beneath a golden veil,
Bright as the rippling ocean in sunshine :
And on the ground, flashing whene'er she stepped,
Beneath her feet the dazzling lightnings leapt
From the gold network of her sandals fine.

26.

Thus Hera stood in royal guise bedecked
Before poor Psyche on the stair that knelt,
Whose new-nursed hope at that display was checked,
And all her happier thoughts gan fade and melt.
She saw no kindnefs in such haughty mien,
And venturing not to look upon the queen,
Bowed down in woe to hear her sentence dealt.

27.

And thus the goddefs spake, " In vain thou suest,
Most miserable Psyche ; though my heart
Be full of hate for her whose hate thou ruest,

And pride and pity move me to thy part:
Yet not till Zeus make known his will, could I,
Least of the blamelefs gods that dwell on high,
Afsist thee, wert thou worthier than thou art.

28.

" But know if Eros love thee, that thy hopes
Should rest on him ; and I would bid thee go
To where within his mother's house he mopes
Apart for lofs of thee in secret woe :
For should he take thee back there is no power
In earth or heaven will hurt thee from that hour,
Nay, not if Zeus himself should prove thy foe."

29.

Thus saying she was gone, and Psyche now
Surprised by comfort rose and went her way,
Resolved in heart, and only wondering how
'Twas pofsible to come where Eros lay ;
Since that her feet, however she might roam,
Could never travel to the heavenly home
Of Love, beyond the bounds of mortal day :

30.

Yet must she come to him.   And now 'twas proved
How that to Lovers, as is told in song,
Seeking the way no place is far removed ;
Nor is there any obstacle so strong,
Nor bar so fixed that it can hinder them :
And how to reach heaven's gate by stratagem
Vexed not the venturous heart of Psyche long.

31.

To face her enemy might well avail :
Wherefore to Cypris' shrine her steps she bent,
Hoping the goddefs in her hate might hale
Her body to the skies for punishment,
Whate'er to be ; yet now her fiercest wrath
Seemed happiest fortune, seeing 'twas the path
Whereby alone unto her love she went.

MEASURE IX.

1.

BUT Aphrodite to the house of Zeus
Being bound, bade now call out her
milkwhite steeds,
Four doves, that ready to her royal use
In golden cages stood and pecked the seeds :
Best of the hundred prisoned birds she broke,
That wore with pride the markings of her yoke,
And cooed in envy of her gentle needs.

2.

These drew in turn her chariot, when in state
Along the heaven with all her train she fared ;
And oft in journeying to the skiey gate
Of Zeus's palace high their flight had dared,
Which darkest vapour and thick glooms enshroud
Above all else in the perpetual cloud,
Wherethro' to mount again they stood prepared,

3.

In twin pairs yokèd to her shining car ;
The same Hephæstos wrought for her, when he,
Bruised in his hideous fall from heaven afar,
Was nursed by Thetis, and Eurynomè,
The daughter of the ever-refluent main ;
With whom he dwelt till he grew sound again,
Down in a hollow cave beside the sea:

4.

And them for kindnefs done was prompt to serve,
Forging them brooches rich in make and mode,
Earrings, and supple chains of jointed curve,
And other trinkets, while he there abode:
And none of gods or men knew of his home,
But they two only ; and the salt sea foam
To and fro past his cavern ever flowed.

5.

'Twas then he wrought this work within the cave,
Embofsed with rich design, a moonèd car ;
And when returned to heaven to Cypris gave,

In form imagined like her crescent star;
Which circling nearest earth, maketh at night
To wakeful mortal men shadow and light
Alone of all the stars in heaven that are.

6.

Two slender wheels it had, with fretted tires
Of biting adamant, to take firm hold
Of cloud or ether; and their whirling fires
Threw off the air in mist where'er they rolled:
And either nave that round the axle turned
A ruby was, whose steady crimson burned
Betwixt the twin speed-mingling fans of gold.

7.

And now the goddefs stood thereon, and shook
The reins; whereat the doves their wings outspread
And rising high their flight to heaven they took:
And all the birds, that in those courts were bred,
Of her broad eaves the nested families,
Sparrows and Swallows joined their companies
Awhile and twittered to her overhead.

8.

But onward she with fading tracks of flame
Sped swiftly, till she reached her journey's end :
And when within the house of Zeus she came,
She prayed the Sire of Heaven that he would lend
Hermes, the Argus-slayer, for her hest;
And he being granted her at her request,
She went forthwith to seek him and to send.

9.

Who happed within the palace then to wait
Upon his master's pleasure ; and her tale
Was quickly told, and he made answer straight
That he would find the truant without fail ;
Asking the goddeſs by what signs her slave
Might best be known, and what the price she gave
For capture, or admitted for the bail.

10.

All which he took his silver stile to write
In letters large upon a waxèd board ;
Her name and colour, features, age, and height,

Her home, and parentage, and the reward :
And then read o'er as 'twas to be proclaimed.
And she took oath to give the price she named,
Without demur, when Psyche was restored.

11.

Then on his head he closely set his cap
With earèd wings erect, and o'er his knee
He crofsed each foot in turn to prove the strap
That bound his winged sandals, and shook free
His chlamys, and gat up, and in his hand
Taking his fair white-ribboned herald's wand,
Leapt forth on air, accoutred cap-a-pè.

12.

And piloting along the mid-day skies
Held southward, till the narrow map of Crete
Lay like a fleck in azure 'neath his eyes;
When down he came, and as an eagle fleet
Drops in some combe, and not till lowest stoop
Spreads wing for check, skimming in level swoop
To strike the bleating quarry with its feet,

13.

Thus he alighted; and in every town
In all the islé before the close of day
Had cried the meſsage, which he carried down,
Of Psyche, Aphrodite's runaway;
That whosoever found the same and caught,
And by such time unto her temple brought,
To him the goddeſs would this guerdon pay:

14.

Six honied kiſses from her rosy mouth
Would Cytherea give, and one beside
To quench at heart for aye love's mortal drouth:
But unto him that hid her, Woe betide!
Which now was on all tongues, and Psyche's name
Herself o'erheard, or ever nigh she came
To Aphrodite's temple where she hied.

15.

When since she found her way to heaven was safe,
She only wished to make it soon and sure;
Nor feared to meet the goddeſs in her chafe,

So she her self-surrender might secure,
And not be given of other for the price;
Nor was her temper apt to use device
Of wit or prudence to conceal her lure.

16.

But now so changed she was by heavy woe,
As not to fear her true description, nor
That such as once had known her now would know;
And when within the fane she stood before
The priestefs and in full herself betrayed,
Scarce could she then with prayer or oath persuade
She was that Psyche known so well of yore.

17.

But when to Hermes she was shown and given,
He took no doubt, but eager to be quit,
And proud of speed, returned with her to heaven,
And left her with the proclamation writ,
Hung at her neck, the board with letters large,
At Aphrodite's gate with those in charge ;
And up whence first he came made haste to flit.

18.

But haplefs Psyche fell, for so it chanced,
To moody Synethea's care, the one
Of Aphrodite's train whom she advanced
To try the work abandoned by her son.
Who by perpetual presence made ill end
Of good or bad; though she could both amend,
And shewed her skill in work by her begun.

19.

But she to such kind thoughts her heart had shut,
And proved she had a spite beyond compare:
Nor could the keenest taunts her anger glut,
Which she when soured was never wont to spare:
But mocking Psyche's shame and pain and grief,
She beat her cruelly, and to her chief
Along the courtyard dragged her by the hair.

20.

Nor now was Aphrodite kinder grown;
But, seeing her she hated in her power,
She laughed for joy, and in triumphant tone

Bade her a merry welcome to her bower :
"'Tis fit indeed daughters-in-law should wait
Upon their mothers ; but thou comest late,
Psyche ; I looked for thee before this hour.

21.

"And yet," thus gave she rein to jeer and gibe,
" Forgive me if I held thee negligent,
Or if accustomed vanity ascribe
An honour to myself was never meant.
Thy lover is it, who so dearly prized
The pretty soul, then left her and despised ?
To him more like thy heavenward steps were bent.

22.

" Nor without reason : Zeus, I tell thee, swooned
To hear the story of the drop of oil,
The revelation and the ghastly wound :
My merriment is but my fear's recoil.
But if my son was unkind, thou shalt see
How kind a goddefs can his mother be
To bring thy tainted honour clear of soil."

I

23.

And so, to match her promise with her mirth,
Two of her ministers she called in ken,
That work the melancholy of the earth ;
Merimna that with care perplexes, when
The hearts of mortals have the gods forgot,
And Lypè, that her sorrow spares them not,
When mortals have forgot their fellow men.

24.

These, like twin sharks that in a fair ship's wake
Swim constant, showing 'bove the water blue
Their shearing fins, and hasty ravin make
Of overthrow or offal, so these two
On Aphrodite's pasing follow hard ;
And now she offered to their glut's regard
Sweet Psyche, with command their wont to do.

25.

But in what secret chamber their foul task
These soul-tormentors plied, or what their skill,
Pity of tender nature may not ask,

Nor poet stain his rhyme with such an ill.
But they at last themselves turned from their rack
Weary of cruelty, and led her back,
Saying that further torture were to kill.

26.

Then when the goddefs saw her, more she mocked
"Art thou the woman of the earth," she said,
That hast in sorceries mine Eros locked,
And stood thyself for worship in my stead ?
Looking that I should pity thee, or care
For what illicit offspring thou mayst bear;
Or let thee to that god my son be wed ?

27.

"I know thy trick; and thou art one of them
Who steal love's favour in the gentle way,
Wearing submifsion for a diadem,
Patience and suffering for thy rich array :
Thou wilt be modest, kind, implicit, so
To rest thy wily spirit out of shew,
That it may leap the livelier into play :

28.

" Devout at doing nothing, if so be
The grace become thee well; but active yet
Above all others be there none to see
Thy businefs, and thine eager face asweat.
Lo! I will prove thy talent: thou mayst live,
And all thou now desirest will I give,
If thou perform the task which I shall set."

29.

She took her then aside, and bade her heed
A heap of grains piled high upon the floor,
Millet and mustard, hemp and poppy seed,
And fern-bloom's undistinguishable spore,
All kinds of pulse, of grafses, and of spice,
Clover and linseed, rape, and corn, and rice,
Dodder, and sesame, and many more.

30.

" Sort me these seeds " she said, " it now is night,
I will return at morning; if I find
That thou hast separated all aright,

Each grain from other grain after its kind,
And set them in unmingled heaps apart,
Then shall thy wish be granted to thine heart."
Whereat she turned, and closed the door behind.

MEASURE X.

1.

A SINGLE lamp there stood beside the heap,
   And shed thereon its mocking golden
      light;
Such as might tempt the weary eye to sleep
Rather than prick the sense of taskèd sight.
Yet Psyche, not to fail for lack of zeal,
With good will set her down to her ordeal,
Sorting the larger seeds as best she might.

2.

When lo! upon the wall, a shadow pafsed
Of doubtful shape, acrofs the chamber dim
Moving with speed: and seeing nought that cast

The shade, she bent her down the flame to trim;
And there the beast itself, a little ant,
Climbed up in compaſs of the lustre scant,
Upon the bowl of oil ran round the rim.

3.

Smiling to see the creature of her fear
So dwarfed by truth, she watched him where he
For mere distraction telling in his ear   [crept,
What straits she then was in, and telling wept.
Whereat he stood and trimmed his horns; but ere
Her tale was done resumed his manner scare,
Ran down, and on his way in darkneſs kept.

4.

But she intent drew forth with dextrous hand
The larger seeds, or pushed the smaller back,
Or light from heavy with her breathing fanned.
When suddenly she saw the floor grow black,
And troops of ants, flowing in noiseleſs train,
Moved to the hill of seeds, as o'er a plain
Armies approach a city for attack;

5.

And gathering on the grain, began to strive
With grappling horns; and each from out the heap
His burden drew, and all their motion live
Struggled and slid upon the surface steep.
And Psyche wondered, watching them, to find
The creatures separated kind from kind :
Till dizzied with the sight she fell asleep.

6.

And when she woke 'twas with the morning sound
Of Aphrodite's anger at the door,
Whom high amaze stayed backward, as she found
Her foe asleep with all her trouble o'er :
And round the room beheld, in order due,
The piles arranged distinct and sorted true,
Grain with grain, seed with seed, and spore with spore.

7.

She fiercely cried " Thou shalt not thus escape ;
For to this marvel dar'st thou not pretend.
There is but one that could this order shape,

Demeter,—but I knew her not thy friend.
Therefore another trial will I set,
In which she cannot aid thee nor abet,
But thou thyself must bring it fair to end."

8.

Thereon she sped her to the bounds of Thrace,
And set her by a river deep and wide,
And said " To east beyond this stream, a race
Of golden-fleecèd sheep at pasture bide.
Go seek them out; and this thy task, to pull
But one lock for me of their precious wool,
And give it in my hands at eventide :

9.

" This do and thou shalt have thy heart's desire.'
Which said, she fled and left her by the stream:
And Psyche then, with courage still entire
Had plunged therein ; but now of great esteem
Her life she rated, while it lent a spell
Wherein she yet might hope to quit her well,
And in one winning all her woes redeem.

10.

There as she stood in doubt, a fluting voice
Rose from the flood, " Psyche, be not afraid
To hear a reed give tongue, for 'twas of choice
That I from mortal flesh a plant was made.
My name is Syrinx ; once from mighty Pan
Into the drowning river as I ran
The change I begged my steps for ever stayed.

11.

" But for that change in many climes I live ;
And Pan, my lover, who to me alone
Is true and does me honour, I forgive—
Nor if I speak in sorrow is't my own :
Rather for thee my voice I now uplift
To warn thee plunge not in the river swift,
Nor seek the golden sheep to men unknown.

12.

" If thou shouldst crofs the stream, which may not be,
Thou couldst not climb upon the hanging rocks,
Nor ever, as the goddefs bade thee, see

The pastures of the yellow-fleecèd flocks :
Or if thou couldst, their herded horns would gore
And slay thee on the crags, or thrust thee o'er
Ere thou couldst rob them of their golden locks.

13.

"The goddeſs means thy death.   But I can show
How thy obedience yet may thwart her will.
At noon the golden flocks descend below,
Leaving the scented herbage of the hill,
And where the shelving banks to shallows fall,
Drink at the rippling waters one and all,
Nor back return till they have drawn their fill.

14.

"I will command a thornbush, that it stoop
Over some ram that steppeth by in peace,
And him in all its prickles firmly coop,
Making thee seizure of his golden fleece ;
So without peril of his angry horns
Shall thou be quit : for he upon the thorns
Must leave his ransom ere he win release."

15.

Then Psyche thanked her for her kind befriending,
And hid among the rushes looking east;
And when noon came she saw the flock descending
Out of the hills; and, lo! one golden beast
Caught in a thornbush; and the mighty brute
Struggled and tore it from its twisted root
Into the stream, or e'er he was released.

16.

And when they watered were and gone, the breeze
Floated the freighted thorn where Psyche lay:
Whence she unhooked the golden wool at ease,
And back to heaven for paſsage swift gan pray.
And Hermes, who was sent to be her guide
Ifso she lived, came down at eventide,
And bore her thither ere the close of day.

17.

But when the goddeſs saw the locks of gold
Held to her hands, her heart with wrath o'erran:
" Most desperate thou, and by abetting bold,

That dost outwit me prove thee as I can.
Yet this work is not thine: there is but one
Of all the gods who could the thing have done.
Hast thou a friend too in the lusty Pan?

18.

"I'll give thee trial where he cannot aid."
Which said, she led her to a torrid land,
Level and black, but not with flood or shade,
For nothing could the mighty heat withstand,
Which aye from morn till eve the naked sun
Poured on that plain, where never foot had run,
Nor any herb sprung on its molten sand.

19.

Far off a gloomy mountain rose alone:
And Aphrodite, thither pointing, said
"There lies thy task. Out of the topmost stone
Of yonder hill upwells a fountain head.
Take thou this goblet; brimming must thou bring
Its cup with water from that sacred spring,
If ever to my son thou wouldst be wed."

20.

Saying, she gave into her hands a bowl
Cut of one crystal, open broad and fair;
And bade her at all hazard keep it whole,
For heaven held nought beside so fine or rare.
Then was she gone; and Psyche on the plain
Now doubted if she ever should regain
The love of Eros, strove she howsoe'er.

21.

Yet as a helmsman, at the word to tack,
Swiftly without a thought puts down his helm,
So Psyche turned to tread that desert black,
Since was no fear that could her heart o'erwhelm;
Nor yet she knew the fount she went to seek
Was cold Cocytus, springing to the peak,
Secretly from his source in Pluto's realm.

22.

All night and day she journeyed, and at last
Come to the rock gazed up in vain around:
For nought she saw but precipices vast

O'er ruined scarps, with rugged ridges crowned,
And sitting down to rest her in the shade,
Or e'er the desperate venture she afsayed,
She fell asleep upon the stony ground.

23.

A dream came to her, thus : she stood alone
Within her palace in the high ravine ;
Where nought but she was changed, but she to stone.
Worshippers thronged the court, and still were seen
Folk flying from the peak, who, ever more
Flying and flying, lighted on the floor,
Hail! cried they, *wife of Eros, adorèd queen!*

24.

A hurtling of the battled air disturbed
Her sunken sense, and waked her eyes to meet
The kingly bird of Zeus, himself that curbed
His swooping course, alighting at her feet ;
With motion gentle, his far darting eye
In kindnefs dimmed upon her, he drew nigh,
And thus in words unveiled her foe's deceit :

25.

" In vain, poor Psyche, has thou hither striven,
Acrofs the fiery plain toiling so well ;
Cruelly to destruction art thou driven
By her, whose hate thou canst not quit nor quell.
No mortal foot may scale this horrid mount,
And those black waters of its topmost fount
Are guarded by the hornèd snakes of hell.

26.

'' Its little rill is an upleaping jet
Of cold Cocytus, which for ever licks
Earth's base, and when with Acheron 'tis met,
Its waters with that other cannot mix,
Which holds the elemental air difsolved :
But with it in its ceaselefs course revolved
Ifsues unmingled in the lake of Styx.

27.

" The souls of murderers, in guise of fish,
Scream as they swim therein and wail for cold,
Their times of woe determined by the wish

Of them they murdered on the earth of old:
Whom each five years they see, whene'er they make
Their paſsage to the Acherusian lake,
And there release may win from pains condoled.

28.

" For if the pitying ear of them they slew
Be haply piercèd by their voices spare,
Then are they freed from pain; as are some few;
But for the most again they forward fare
To Tartarus obscene, and outcast thence
Are hurried back into the cold intense,
And with new company their torments share.

29.

" Its biting lymph may not be touched of man
Or god, unleſs the Fates have so ordained;
Nor could I in thy favour break the ban,
Nor paſs the dragons that thereby are chained
Didst thou not bear the sacred cup of Zeus;
Which, for thy peril lent, shall turn to use,
And truly do the service which it feigned."

K

30.

Thus as he spake his talons made he ring
Around the crystal bowl, and soaring high
Descended as from heaven upon the spring :
Nor dared the hornèd snakes of hell deny
The minister of Zeus, that bore his cup,
To fill it with their trusted water up,
Thence to the King of heaven therewith to fly.

31.

But he to Psyche bent his gracious speed,
And bidding her to mount his feathered back
Bore her aloft as once young Ganymede;
Nor ever made his steady flight to slack,
Ere that he set her down beside her goal,
And gave into her hands the crystal bowl
Unspilled, o'erbrimming with the water black.

MEASURE XI.

1.

BUT Eros now recovered from his hurt,
Felt other pangs ; for who would not
relent
Weighing the small crime and unmatched desert
Of Psyche with her cruel punishment ?
And shamed he grew to be so near allied
To her, who by her taunts awoke his pride,
As his compaſsion by her spite unspent.

2.

Which Aphrodite seeing waxed more firm
That he should never meet with Psyche more ;
And had in thought already set the term
To their communion with that trial sore,
Which sent her forth upon a quest accursed,
And not to be accomplished, that of thirst
She there might perish on hell's torrid shore.

3.

And now it chanced that she had called her son
Into her presence-chamber, to unfold
Psyche's destruction, that her fate might stun
What love remained by duty uncontrolled;
And he to hide his tears' rebellious storm
Was fled; when in his place another form
Rose 'neath the golden lintel; and behold

4.

Psyche herself, in slow and balanced strain,
Poising the crystal bowl with fearful heed,
Her eyes at watch upon the steadied plane,
And whole soul gathered in the single deed.
Onward she came, and stooping to the floor
Set down the cup unspilled and brimming o'er
At Aphrodite's feet, and rose up freed.

5.

Surprise o'ercame the goddess, and she too
Stood like a statue, but with passion pale:
Till, when her victim nothing spake, she threw

Some kindnefs in her voice, and bade her hail;
But in the smiling judge 'twas plain to see—
Saying " What water bringst thou here to me?"—
That justice over hate should not prevail.

6.

Then Psyche said " This is the biting flood
Of black Cocytus, silvered with the gleam
Of souls, that guilty of another's blood
Are pent therein, and as they swim they scream.
The hornèd snakes of hell, upon the mount
Enchained, for ever guard the livid fount :
And but the Fates can grant to touch the stream."

7.

" Wherefore" the goddefs cried "'tis plain that none
But one I wot of could this thing have wrought.
That which another doth may well be done
Nor thou the nearer to my promise brought.
Thou buildest on a hope to be destroyed,
If thou accept conditions, and avoid
Thy parcel, nor thyself accomplish aught.

8.

" Was it not kindnefs in me, being averse
To all thy wish, to yield me thus to grant
Thy heart's desire,—and nothing loathe I worse,-
If thou wouldst only work as well as want ?
See, now I will not yet be all denial,
But offer thee one last determining trial ;
And let it be a mutual covenant :

9.

" This box," and in her hands she took a pyx
Square-cut, of dark obsidian's rarest green,
" Take ; and therewith beyond Tartarean Styx
Go thou, and entering Hades' house obscene,
Say to Persephonè, *If 'tis thy will*
To show me so much favour, prithee fill
This little vase with beauty for Love's queen.

10.

" *She begs but what shall well o'erlast a day ;* .
For of her own was much of late outspent
In nursing of her son, in bed who lay

Wounded by me, who for the gift am sent.
Then bring me what she gives, and with all speed;
For truth to say I stand, thou seest, in need
Of some such charm in my disparagement.

11.

" If thou return to me with that acquist,
Having thyself the journey made, I swear
That day to give thee whatsoe'er thou list,
And be it my son. Now, Psyche, wilt thou dare?"
And Psyche said " If this thou truly mean,
I will go down to Tartarus obscene,
And beg of Hades' queen thy beauty there.

12.

"Show me the way." But Aphrodite said,
" That mayst thou find. Yet I will place thee whence
A way there is: mortals have on it sped ;
Ay, and returned thereby : so let us hence."
Then swift to earth her willing prey she bore,
And left her on the wide Laconian shore,
Alone, at midnight, in the darkneſs dense.

13.

'Twas winter ; and as shivering Psyche sat
Waiting for morn, she questioned in her mind
What place the goddefs meant, arrived whereat
She might descend to hell, or how should find
The way which Gods to living men deny.
" No Orpheus, nay, nor Heracles am I,"
Said she, " to loosen where the great Gods bind."

14.

And when at length the long delaying dawn
Broke on the peaks of huge Taÿgetus,
And Psyche through the skirts of dark withdrawn.
Looked on that promontory mountainous,
And saw high-crested Taleton in snow,
Her heart sank, and she wept with head bent low
The malice of her foe dispiteous.

15.

And seeing near at hand an ancient tower,
Deserted now, but once a hold of men,
She came thereto, and, though 'twas all her power,

Mounted its steep unbroken stair again.
" Surely," she said, for now a second time
She thought to die—" this little height I climb
Will prove my shortest road to Pluto's den.

16.

" Hence must I come to Tartarus; once there
Turn as I may," and straight to death had sprung;
When in the mofsy tower the imprisoned air
Was shaken, and its hoary stones gave tongue,
"Stand firm! stand firm!" that rugged voice outcried;
" Of such as choose despondency for guide
Hast thou not heard what bitterest fate is sung ?

17.

" Hearken; for I the road and means can teach
How thou mayst come to hell and yet escape.
And first must thou, that upper gate to reach,
Along these seagirt hills thy journey shape,
To where the land in sea dips furthest South
At Tænarus and Hades' earthly mouth,
Hard by Poseidon's temple at the cape.

18.

" Thereby may one descend : but they that make
That paſsage down must go provided well.
So take in either hand a honey-cake
Of pearlèd barley mixed and hydromel ;
And in thy mouth two doits, first having bound
The pyx beneath thy robe enwrapped around :
Thus set thou forth ; and mark what more I tell.

19.

" When thou hast gone alone some half thy road
Thou wilt o'ertake a lame outwearied aſs ;
And one that beats him, tottering 'neath his load
Of logs, and beats in vain, will cry, *Alas ;
Help me, kind friend, my faggots to adjust !*
But thou that silly cripple's words mistrust ;
'Tis planted for thy death.   Note it and paſs.

20.

" And when thy road the Stygian river joins,
Where woolly Charon ferries o'er the dead,
He will demand his fare : one of thy coins

Force with thy tongue between thy teeth, thy head
Offering instead of hand to give the doit.
His fingers in this custom are adroit,
And thine must not set down the barleybread.

21.

" Then in his crazy bark as, ferrying o'er
The stream, thou sittest, one that seems to float
Rather than swim, midway 'twixt shore and shore,
Will stretch his fleshleſs hand upon the boat,
And beg thee of thy pity take him in.
Shut thy soft ear unto his clamour thin,
Nor for a phantom deed thyself devote.

22.

" Next, on the further bank when thou art stepped,
Three wizened women weaving at the woof
Will stop, and pray thee in their art adept
To free their tangled threads.   Hold thou aloof;
For this and other traps thy foe hath planned
To make thee drop the cakes from out thy hand,
Putting thy prudence to perpetual proof.

23.

" For by one cake thou comest into Hell,
And by one cake departest; since the hound
That guards the gate is ever pleasèd well
To taste man's meal, or sweetened grain unground.
Cast him a cake; for that thou mayst go free
Even to the mansion of Persephonè,
Without more stay or peril, safe and sound.

24.

" She will receive thee kindly; thou decline
Her courtesies, and make the floor thy seat;
Refusing all is offered, food or wine;
Save only beg a crust of bread to eat.
Then tell thy mifsion, and her present take;
Which when thou hast, set forth with pyx and cake,
One in each hand, while yet thou mayst retreat.

25.

" Giving thy second cake to Cerberus,
The coin to Charon, and that way whereby
Thou camest following, thou comest thus

To see again the starry choir on high.
But guard thou well the pyx, nor once uplift
The lid to look on Persephaſsa's gift;
Else 'tis in vain I bid thee now not die."

26.

Then Psyche thanked the tower, and stooped her
    mouth
To kiſs the stones upon his rampart hoary;
And coming down his stair went hasting south,
Along the steep Tænarian promontory :
And found the cave and temple by the cape,
And took the cakes and coins, and made escape
Beneath the earth, according to his story.

27.

And overtook the aſs, but lent no aid ;
And offered Charon with her teeth his fee;
And paſsed the floating ghost, in vain who prayed;
And turned her back upon the weavers three :
And threw the cake he loved to that hell-hound
Three-headed Cerberus; and safe and sound,
Came to the mansion of Persephonè.

28.

Kindly received she courtesy declined;
Sat on the ground; ate not, save where she lay
A crust of bread; revealed the goddeſs' mind;
The gift took; and returned upon her way:
Gave Cerberus his cake, Charon his fare,
And saw through Hell's mouth to the purple air
And one by one the keen stars melt in day.

29.

Awhile from so long journeying in the shades
Resting at Tænarus she came to know
How, on the eastern coast, some forty stades,
There stood a temple of her goddeſs foe.
There would she make her offering, there reclaim
The prize, which now 'twas happineſs to name,
The joy that should redeem all paſsèd woe.

30.

And wending by the sunny shore at noon,
She with her pyx, and wondering what it hid,
Of what kind, what the fashion of the boon

She carried, but to look on was forbid,—
Alas for Innocence so hard to teach !—
At fancy's prick she sat her on the beach,
And to content desire lifted the lid.

31.

She saw within nothing : But o'er her sight
That looked on nothing gan a darkneſs creep.
A cloudy poison, mixed of Stygian night,
Rapt her to deadly and infernal sleep.
Backward she fell, like one when all is o'er,
And lay outstretched, as lies upon the shore
A drowned corpse cast up by the murmuring deep.

MEASURE XII.

1.

WHILE Eros in his chamber hid his tears,
Mourning the lofs of Psyche and her fate,
The rumour of her safety reached his ears
And how she came to Aphrodite's gate :
Whereat with hope returned his hardihood,
And secretly he purposed while he could
Himself to save her from the goddefs' hate.

2.

Then learning what he might and guefsing more,
His ready wit came soon to understand
The journey to the far Laconian shore ;

Whither to fly and seek his love he planned :
And making good escape in dark of night,
Ere the sun crofsed his true meridian flight
He by Teuthronè struck the southern strand.

3.

There as it chanced he found that snowy bird
Of Crete, that late made mischief with his queen,
And now along the cliffs with wings unstirred
Sailed, and that morn had crofsed the sea between
Whom as he pafsed he hailed, and questioned thus
"O snowy gull, if thou from Tænarus
Be come, say, hast thou there my Psyche seen?"

4.

The gull replied " Thy Psyche have I seen;
Walking beside the sea she joys to bear
A pyx of dark obsidian's rarest green,
Wherein she gazes on her features fair.
She is not hence by now six miles at most."
Then Eros bade him speed, and down the coast
Held on his pafsage through the buoyant air.

L

5.

With eager eye he searched the salty marge,
Boding all mischief from his mother's glee;
And wondering of her wiles, and what the charge
Shut in the dark obsidian pyx might be.
And lo! at last, outstretched beside the rocks,
Psyche as lifeless; and the open box
Laid with the weedy refuse of the sea.

6.

He guessed all, flew down, and beside her knelt,
With both his hands stroking her temples wan;
And for the poison with his fingers felt,
And drew it gently from her; and anon
She slowly from those Stygian fumes was freed;
Which he with magic handling and good heed
Replaced in pyx, and shut the lid thereon.

7.

" O Psyche," thus, and kissing her he cried,
" O simple-hearted Psyche, once again
Hast thou thy foolish longing gratified,

A second time hath prying been thy bane.
But lo! I, love, am come, for I am thine:
Nor ever more shall any fate malign,
Or spite of goddefs smite our love in twain.

8.

" Let now that I have saved thee twice outweigh
The once that I deserted thee : and thou
Hast much obeyed for once to disobey,
And wilt no more my bidding disallow.
Take up thy pyx; to Aphrodite go,
And claim the promise of thy mighty foe;
Maybe that she will grant it to thee now.

9.

" If she refuse, and still from pity lean,
Despair not yet."   Then swiftly to the sky
He sped with Psyche, setting her unseen
At Aphrodite's golden gate, whereby
They came as night was close on twilight dim :
But Eros, bidding her speak nought of him,
Flew to the house of Zeus on purpose high.

10.

There winning audience of the heavenly sire,
Who well disposed to him was used to be,
He told the story of his strong desire ;
And boldly begged that Zeus would grant his plea,
That he might have sweet Psyche for his wife,
And she be dowered with immortal life,
Since she was worthy, by his firm decree.

11.

And great Zeus smiled ; and at the smile of Zeus
All heaven was glad, and on the earth below
Was calm and peace awhile and sorrow's truce :
The sun shone forth and smote the winter snow,
The flowërs sprang, the birds gan sing and pair,
And mortals, as they drew the brightened air
Marvelled, and quite forgot their common woe.

12.

Yet gave the Thunderer not his full consent
Without some words : "At length is come the day,"
Thus spake he, " when for all thy youth mifspent,

Thy mischief-making and thy wanton play
Thou art upgrown to taste the sweet and sour.   ·
Good shall it work upon thee : from this hour
Look we for better things.   And this I say,

13.

"That since thy birth, which all we took for blifs,
Thou hast but mocked us ; and no lefs on me
Hast brought disfavour and contempt ywifs,
Than others that have had to do with thee :
Till only such as vowed themselves aloof
From thee and thine were held in good aproof;
And few there were, who thus of shame went free.

14.

"That punishment is shapen as reward
Is like thy fortune : but our good estate
We honour, while we sit to be adored :
And thus 'twas written in the book of Fate.
Not for thy pleasure, but the general weal
Grant I the grace for which thou here dost kneel ;
And that which I determine shall not wait."

15.

So winged Hermes through the heaven he sped,
To warn the high celestials to his hall,
Where they should Eros see with Psyche wed,
And keep the day with feast ambrosial.
And Hermes, flying through the skiey ways
Of high Olympus, spread sweet Psyche's praise,
And bade the mighty gods obey his call.

16.

Then all the Kronian gods and goddefses
Afsembled at his cry,—and now 'twas known
Why Zeus had smiled,—the lefser majesties
Attending them before his royal throne.
Athena, mistrefs good of them that know,
Came, and Apollo, warder off of woe,
Who had to Psyche's sire her fate foretold,

17.

Demeter, giver of the golden corn,
Fair Hebe, honoured at her Attic shrine,
And Artemis with hunting spear and horn,

And Dionysos, planter of the vine
With old Poseidon from the barren sea,
And Leto, and the lame Hephestos, he
Himself who built those halls with skill divine.

18.

And ruddy Pan with many a quip and quirk
Aired mong those lofty gods his mirth illbred,
Bearing a mighty bowl of cretan work,
Stern Arês with his crisp hair helmeted,
And grave retirèd Hestia, and the god
Hermes, with wingèd cap and ribboned rod,
By whom the company was heralded.

19.

And Hera sat by Zeus, and all around
The Muses, that of learning make their choice;
Who, when Apollo struck his strings to sound,
Sang in alternate music with sweet voice :
And righteous Themis, and the Graces three
Followed, and Aphrodite last, for she
Alone of all were there might not rejoice.

20.

But at the banquet ere they sat to feast
Zeus spake, and said " This marriage here to make
Stays, from one hindrance first to be released,
For Arês' and for Aphrodite's sake,
Nay, for our common honour, lest their son,
Who is as one of us, should mate with one
That doth not of our heavenly life partake.

21.

" Wherefore my purpose is that Psyche drink
The cup ambrosial of immortal life,
Which if we grant, the goddefs, as I think,
Will not forbid her then for Eros' wife.
Thus the mislike and discord, which had birth
From too great honour, paid the bride on earth,
May end, and therewithal all further strife."

22.

Then Aphrodite said " So let it be."
And Psyche was brought in, with such a flush
Of joy upon her face, as there to see

Was fairer to love's eye than beauty's blush.
And then she drank the eternal wine, whose draught
Can Terror cease : which flesh hath never quaffed,
Nor doth it flow from grapes that mortals crush.

23.

And next stood Eros forth, and took her hand,
And kifsed her happy face before them all :
And Zeus proclaimed them married, and outbanned
From heaven whoever should that word miscall.
And then all sat to feast, and one by one
Pledged Psyche ere they drank and cried *Well done !*
And merry laughter rang throughout the hall.

24.

So thus was Eros unto Psyche wed,
The heavenly bridegroom to his earthly bride,
Who won his love, in simple maidenhead :
And by her love herself she glorified,
And him from wanton wildnefs disinclined ;
Since in his love for her he came to find
A joy unknown through all Olympus wide.

25.

And Psyche for her fall was quite forgiven,
Since 'gainst herself when tempted to rebel,
By others' malice on her ruin driven,
Only of sweet simplicity she fell :—
Wherein who fall may fall unto the skies;—
And being foolish she was yet most wise,
And took her trials patiently and well.

26.

And Aphrodite since her full defeat
Is kinder and less jealous than before,
And smiling on them both, calls Psyche sweet;
But thinks her son less manly than of yore :
Though still she holds his arm of some renown,
When he goes smiting mortals up and down,
'Piercing their marrow with his weapons sore.

27.

So now in steadfast love and happy state
They hold for aye their mansions in the sky,
And kindly look on those in love who mate,

And seek the peace themselves have won thereby :
Whom gently Eros shooteth, and apart
Keepeth for them from all his sheaf that dart
Which Psyche in his chamber picked to try.

28.

Now in that same month Psyche bare a child,
Who straight in heaven was naméd Hedonè
In mortal tongues by other letters styled ;
Whom all to love, however named, agree :
Whom in our noble English JOY we call,
And honour them among us most of all,
Whose happy children are as fair as she.

L'ENVOY.

It is my prayer that she may smile on all
Who read my tale as she hath smiled on me.

YATTENDON,

June 30, 1884.

NOTE.

The foregoing poem pretends neither to originality nor loftiness. The beautiful story is well known, and the version of Apuleius has been simply followed. Such variations and ornament as are introduced perhaps fall short of what a poetic reader might expect from a poet of this time. The location of the fable, a gentler handling of motive, and the substitution of Hellenism for latin vulgarity are examples of these liberties, which will be readily allowed; and this last in spite of matter in the story which would support the opinion that the Greek mind can have mingled but little in the authorship. If the consequent inconsistency should offend scholars they are requested to consider the insipidity of the alternative. The introduction of art into the palace of Eros is not intended to imply that he himself had delight in it, or understanding of it; the palace was for Psyche's satisfaction: but it may be doubted whether the works described are proper creations of Olympian or supermundane intelligence. The alternative is again insipid ; and the dull furniture of Apuleius is probably an accident of the oriental source of the story ; but the addition made to Homer's description of Hera's drefs is an orientalism of the present writer. On the other hand, a reader unacquainted with the clafsics is warned that many beauties of the poem are borrowed plumes ; and in the absence of notes it may be well to refer generally to Father Homer, Pindar, Plato, Moschus, Callimachus, the Greek anthology, Lucian, Lucretius, Virgil, Dante (but let the reader of Dante observe that XI. 25. 4 is a literal translation of Apuleius), Petrarch, Botticelli, Titian, Rafael, Spenser (from whom the first line of XII. 27 is transcribed in homage to his account of " Cupid and Psyche" in the Fairy Queen), Wyatt, the mighty Shakespeare and others. The author has never read any English version of the story. The metre he has used before ; it is in his opinion the most pleasing form of the seven-line stanza, though hitherto neglected. The prosody is in the inconsistent manner of the seventeenth century. As for the mediocrity of the verses attributed to Apollo, the responsibility lies with the god, the Pythoneſs, Apuleius, or his old woman. The present translator may claim to have done them all a good turn by reducing their oracle from eight to seven lines.

He has lastly to acknowledge the kindneſs of friends, some of whom have criticized and some amended his poem, while others now have persuaded him to allow them to publish it. For his own legion faults he begs the reader's indulgence.

October, 1885.

CHISWICK PRESS :—C. WHITTINGHAM AND CO., TOOKS COURT,
CHANCERY LANE.

ImTheStory.com

CPSIA information can be obtained at www.ICGtesting.com
Printed in the USA
BVOW06s1123191016

465444BV00009B/83/P

9 781313 140836